Recipes and food styling by Valéry Drouet
Photos by Pierre-Louis Viel

All the recipes in the 'Grilled' section have been designed for cooking on a plancha grill. This method of cooking on a metal plate or *plancha* (Spanish for 'metal plate') creates a very hot and even surface. It is also an energy efficient and healthy method of grilling. A griddle or shallow stovetop grill pan are good alternatives.

VALÉRY DROUET & PIERRE-LOUIS VIEL

FISH & MORE

[FISH AND SEAFOOD TO GRILL OR COOK]

CONTENTS

OVEN-BAKED

Fish

Shellfish

SAUCES

TARTARE SAUCE

HOLLANDAISE SAUCE

ROUILLE

FISH VELOUTÉ

BEURRE BLANC

SHELLFISH BISQUE

All recipes are for 6 persons.

TARTARE SAUCE

》 Chop 2 hard-boiled eggs, 1 oz (30 g) capers, 6 large cornichons, 2 green onions, and 1 small bunch of chervil. Mix all the ingredients together in a bowl with 1 cup (250 ml) mayonnaise.

Serve with grilled fish.

HOLLANDAISE SAUCE

》 Melt 1 $\frac{1}{3}$ cups (300 g) butter in a double boiler. When the butter has melted, clarify by skimming off the curd that has formed on the surface and other impurities. Mix 5 egg yolks with 3 tablespoons (45 ml) water in a pan. Heat gently for 6–8 minutes, beating continuously to produce a light frothy sauce. Remove pan from heat and beat in the clarified butter. Add the juice of ½ lemon and salt and pepper. Keep the sauce at room temperature.

Goes well with, for instance, salmon noisettes with Roquefort (p. 26), sardines with herb pesto (p. 44), salmon patties with bacon and onion (p. 57), or monkfish with grilled leeks and red onions (p. 60).

ROUILLE

》 Using a food processor, combine 1 cooked egg yolk, 1 raw egg yolk, 1 tablespoon mustard, 1 anchovy fillet, 1 large clove garlic (peeled), 2 pinches saffron, 2 pinches ground paprika, 1 teaspoon tomato purée, and salt and pepper to taste.

》 Whizz for 30 seconds, then add 7 tablespoons (100 ml) each of olive and sunflower oil.

》 Whizz again for a few seconds until the sauce is nice and smooth.

Serve with fish soup (see recipe p. 136), or with grilled fish.

FISH VELOUTÉ

» In a saucepan, boil 1¾ cups (400 ml) fish stock until reduced by half. Add a generous ¾ cup (200 ml) heavy cream and season with salt and pepper. Reduce again until you have a moderately thick sauce. Beat in 4 tablespoons (60 g) chilled butter and boil for 2 minutes. Whizz the mixture with a hand blender until smooth and creamy. Keep it warm in a double boiler.

Before serving, you can add some chopped chives, curry powder, saffron, mustard seeds, or sea urchin paste

BEURRE BLANC

» In a small saucepan, boil scant 1 cup (200 ml) white wine with 2 chopped shallots and a sprig of thyme until almost completely reduced. Add scant 1 cup (200 ml) heavy cream and reduce by half again. Remove from heat and mix in 14 tablespoons (200 g) finely diced chilled butter, beating continuously. Pass the beurre blanc through a sieve and keep hot in a double boiler.

Serve with grilled haddock in horseradish marinade (p. 16), chunky cod fillets with chorizo (p. 25), or scallop skewers with shiitake mushrooms (p. 66).

SHELLFISH BISQUE

» Put 3½ tablespoons (50 ml) olive oil in a large pan and sweat 2 carrots, 2 garlic cloves, and 2 onions, all finely chopped. Add 2¼ lb (1 kg) crushed shells of crab or other crustaceans, and sear for 5 minutes, stirring well. Mix in generous 1 tablespoon (20 g) tomato purée and brown for 2 minutes. Flambé the mixture with 1 small glass cognac. Cover well with water, then add 3 chopped tomatoes, salt, and pepper. Bring to a boil and cook over medium heat for 1 hour.

» Whizz with a hand blender for 2 minutes, then pass through a fine sieve, pressing down well to extract as much liquid as possible. Pour into a pan. Add scant 1 cup (200 ml) heavy cream, salt, and pepper. Cook for 15 minutes over medium heat. Remove pan from heat, then beat in 2 tablespoons (30 g) chilled butter. Whisk the bisque with a hand blender and serve piping hot.

Serve with crab cakes with garlic and chili (p. 89), roast turbot in bacon, with lettuce and peas (p. 104), or langoustines (p. 132).

Fish stock

INGREDIENTS

Makes approx. 2½ cups (600 ml) stock

- 1¾ lb (800 g) fish bones (preferably flat fish such as turbot, sole, or John Dory)
- 4 shallots, finely chopped
- 2 tbsp (30 g) butter
- 1¼ cups (300 ml) white wine

》 Chop the bones into small pieces and rinse under cold water. In a large pan, sweat the shallots in the butter over medium heat. Add the bones and brown for 5 minutes.

》 Pour in the white wine and top up with enough cold water to cover the bones. Bring to a boil and cook for 20 minutes over medium heat, skimming the surface occasionally. Strain the fish stock through a fine sieve.

Use the stock within 48 hours, or store in the freezer in small plastic containers. You can even make fish stock ice cubes, which are very practical if you just need small amounts.

Court-bouillon with white wine

INGREDIENTS

Makes 3 quarts (3 liters) of court-bouillon

- 1 carrot
- 1 large onion
- 2 cups (500 ml) white wine
- 2½ quarts (2½ liters) water
- 1 sprig rosemary
- 2 sprig thyme
- 3 slices lemon
- 1 tbsp coarse salt
- 15 peppercorns

》 Peel and finely slice the onion and carrot.

》 Pour the water and white wine into a pan. Add the sliced onion and carrot, lemon slices, thyme, rosemary, and salt. Bring to a boil and cook for 15 minutes over medium heat. Remove from heat, add the peppercorns, and leave to cool completely. Strain the court-bouillon.

》 For this cooking method, place the fish in a large, deep dish or baking tray (suitable for the stovetop) and cover with the cold court-bouillon. Bring slowly to a boil and cook gently for 10–20 minutes (depending on the size and type of fish). Depending on the recipe you are using, drain the fish if serving it hot, or leave it to cool in the court-bouillon.

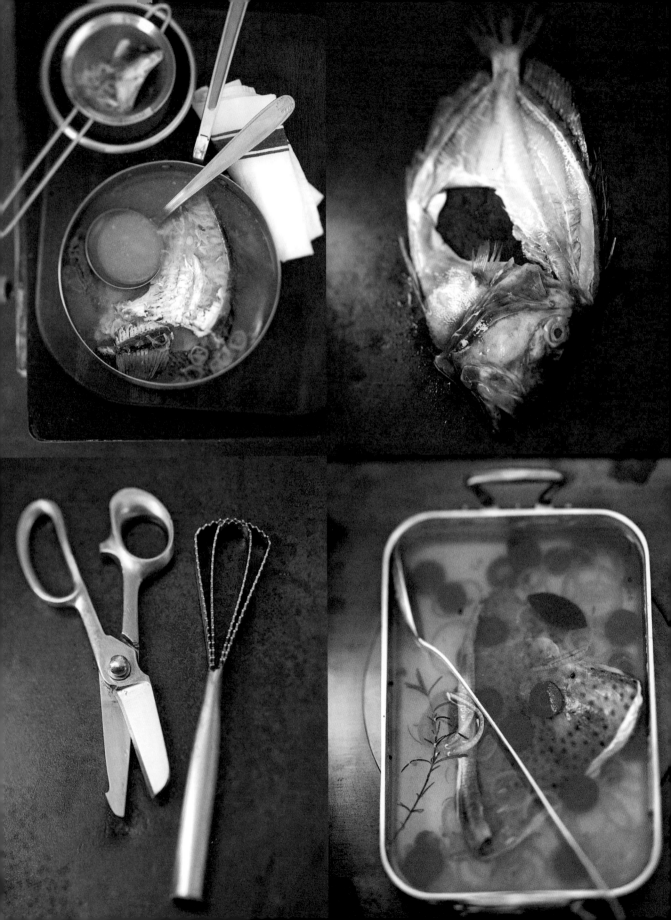

GRILLED

GRILLED HADDOCK WITH HORSERADISH MARINADE

PREPARATION : **30 minutes**
MARINADE : **3 hours**
COOKING TIME : **10 minutes**

INGREDIENTS

Serves 6

- 6 chunky haddock fillets, each
  approx. 6 oz (160–180 g)
- 7 tbsp (100 ml) orange juice
- salt, ground pepper
- ²/₃ cup (150 ml) olive oil
- generous 2 tbsp (30 g)
  horseradish
- 1¾ lb (750 g) waxy, red-skinned
  potatoes (e.g. Roseval)
- 3 shallots
- 1 small bunch flat-leaf parsley
- 3 tbsp (45 ml) white wine vinegar

》 Mix the orange juice with salt and pepper in a bowl. Add half of the olive oil and all of the horseradish.

》 Place the haddock fillets in a shallow dish and pour the horseradish marinade over them. Cover the dish with plastic wrap and refrigerate for 3 hours.

》 Wash the potatoes and cook them for 20 minutes in a pan of boiling, salted water.

》 Peel and chop the shallots. Wash and chop the parsley.

》 Combine the vinegar and salt and pepper in a salad bowl. Add the rest of the oil, then the chopped shallots and parsley. Mix all ingredients well.

》 Pre-heat the plancha (see p. 4).

》 Drain, but do not rinse, the potatoes. Cut them into slices and add them to the vinaigrette in the salad bowl.

》 Drain off the marinade, reserving it, and grill the haddock fillets for 5 minutes on each side.

》 Serve the haddock fillets with the warm potatoes and some marinade on the side.

PREPARATION: **45 minutes**
REFRIGERATION: **6 hours**
COOKING TIME: **15 minutes**

MONKFISH WITH BACON AND SAGE

INGREDIENTS

Serves 6

- 6 monkfish fillets, each
  approx. 5½ oz (160 g)
- 2 shallots
- 1 clove garlic
- 13 tbsp (180 g) butter
- 12 sage leaves
- salt, ground pepper
- 12 slices bacon
- 9 green tomatoes
- 1¼ cups (300 ml) fish
  stock (see recipe p. 12)
- 3 tbsp (45 ml) olive oil
  + a small amount for
  grilling

≫ Peel and chop the shallots and garlic. Chop 6 sage leaves.

≫ In a bowl, combine 7 tablespoons of softened butter with the shallots, garlic, chopped sage, and salt and pepper to taste.

≫ Slice each monkfish portion in half to make a pocket. Season the insides, and stuff with half of the sage butter. Close the pockets and smear on the rest of the sage butter. Wrap 2 slices of bacon tightly around each fillet. Cover with plastic wrap and refrigerate for 6 hours.

≫ Chop the remaining sage leaves. Heat up the fish stock in a pan with salt and pepper, and boil for 5 minutes. Beat in the rest of the cold, chopped butter on high heat and then add the chopped sage. Whizz the sauce with a hand blender, and keep it hot without boiling.

≫ Pre-heat and lightly oil the plancha (see p. 4).

≫ Wash the tomatoes and cut them in half. Season with salt and pepper on the cut side, and drizzle with olive oil.

≫ Grill the tomatoes on the flesh sides. At the same time, place the monkfish portions on the plancha and cook for 10—15 minutes, turning frequently. Serve immediately with the sage sauce.

ORIENTAL-STYLE SALMON FILLETS

PREPARATION: **30 minutes**
COOKING TIME: **20 minutes**

INGREDIENTS
Serves 6

- 6 premium quality Scottish salmon fillets, de-scaled, each approx. 6 oz (180 g)
- 7 tbsp (100 ml) olive oil + a small amount for grilling
- 3 zucchini
- 18 chive blades or green onions
- sea salt, ground pepper
- 1 bunch cilantro
- 1 clove garlic
- 1 level tsp coriander seeds
- 1 level tsp cumin powder
- generous 1 tsp harissa paste
- 3 tbsp (45 ml) lemon juice

❯ Pre-heat the plancha (see p. 4) to medium heat and lightly oil it.

❯ Wash the zucchini and slice them into rounds. Wash the chives (or green onions).

❯ Season the salmon fillets with sea salt and pepper, then place them skin side down on the plancha.

❯ Place the zucchini and chives alongside the fish. Cook the fillets on one side, undisturbed, for 15–20 minutes until the flesh becomes translucent. Turn the zucchini and chives a few times so they are grilled all over.

❯ Meanwhile, peel the garlic clove. Wash the cilantro, remove the stalks, and put the leaves in a high-sided bowl. Add the garlic, cumin, coriander seeds, lemon juice, harissa, olive oil, and a pinch of salt. Whizz for 20 seconds with a hand blender.

❯ When the salmon fillets and vegetables are cooked, brush on the Oriental marinade. Serve immediately, with the remaining marinade on the side.

SOLE FILLETS WITH HERB CRUMB

PREPARATION : 40 minutes
COOKING TIME: 10 minutes

INGREDIENTS
Serves 6

- 12 large sole fillets
- 1 bunch flat-leaf parsley
- 1 bunch chervil
- 1 bunch cilantro
- $^2/_3$ cup (150 ml) olive oil + a small amount for grilling
- 1 level tsp pink peppercorns
- 5 oz (140 g) breadcrumbs
- salt, ground pepper
- 2 shallots
- $^2/_3$ cup (150 ml) white wine
- generous ¾ cup (200 ml) heavy cream
- juice of 2 lemons
- $^2/_3$ cup (150 g) butter

≫ Wash the herbs and remove the stalks. Put the leaves in a food processor with 3 tablespoons of olive oil. Add the pink peppercorns, breadcrumbs, and some salt. Blend all the ingredients together until you have slightly moist green crumbs.

≫ Season the sole fillets with salt and pepper and coat them in the green crumb mixture, pressing down well so that it sticks to the fish. Put them in the refrigerator.

≫ Peel and chop the shallots. Put them in a pan with the white wine. Bring to a boil, and reduce until almost dry. Add the cream and reduce by half. Remove from stovetop, beat in the chopped butter, then add the lemon juice, and salt and pepper to taste. Pass the lemon butter through a fine sieve and keep it hot in the bowl of a double boiler.

≫ Pre-heat the plancha (see p. 4) and oil it well.

≫ Cook the crumbed sole fillets on the plancha for 4–5 minutes on each side, basting with the remaining olive oil on both sides as they cook.

≫ Using a hand blender, whizz the warm lemon butter until smooth and creamy. Serve the sole fillets piping hot with the lemon butter, and grilled bell peppers or fragrant rice on the side.

Chunky cod with chorizo and Manchego

PREPARATION : **30 minutes**
COOKING TIME : **45 minutes**

INGREDIENTS

Serves 6

- 6 chunky cod fillets, each approx.
  5½ oz (160 g)
- $^2/_3$ cup (150 ml) olive oil + a small
  amount for grilling
- 4 red bell peppers
- 3 cloves garlic
- 1 small, strongly flavored chorizo
- 7 oz (200 g) Manchego cheese
- 1 level tbsp Espelette pepper
  (mild, smoky chili)
- salt, ground pepper

》 Pre-heat then lightly oil the plancha (see p. 4).

》 Cut the bell peppers into halves or quarters and place them on a sheet of aluminum foil with the unpeeled garlic cloves. Season with salt and pepper, then close and tightly seal the foil to form a parcel, keeping it as flat as possible. Place the foil parcel on the plancha and cook for 25–30 minutes, turning frequently.

》 Meanwhile, slice the cod fillets in half to make a pocket. Season the insides with salt and half of the Espelette pepper.

》 Remove the chorizo skin and slice it into thin rounds. Remove the cheese rind and make shavings using a vegetable peeler.

》 Stuff the cod fillets with the Manchego shavings and chorizo slices. Tie the parcels up with string, pressing together gently. Season the outside with salt and the rest of the Espelette pepper. Lightly oil the fish fillets.

》 Take the foil parcel out of the plancha, remove the bell peppers, and leave to cool slightly before peeling off the skins. Blend the peppers and garlic cloves together with 6–7 tablespoons of hot water, 7–8 tablespoons of olive oil, and salt and pepper, until you have a thick coulis (add a little hot water if it is still too thick).

》 Grill the cod fillets for 6–8 minutes on each side. Serve immediately with the pepper coulis.

SALMON NOISETTES WITH ROQUEFORT

PREPARATION : **30 minutes**
COOKING TIME : **30 minutes**

INGREDIENTS
Serves 6

- 2 lb (900 g) premium quality Scottish salmon fillet, skin removed
- 7½ oz (220 g) Roquefort cheese
- salt, ground pepper
- 9 small endives
- 2 tbsp caraway seeds
- 3 tbsp (45 ml) olive oil

> Cut the salmon fillet into 18 slices, each approx. ½ inch (1.5 cm) thick. Remove any gray flesh.

> Place a piece of Roquefort on each slice. Carefully roll the slices up, pressing together gently, and tie with string to keep them in place. Season each portion with a little salt (the cheese is already salty) and pepper.

> Pre-heat the plancha (see p. 4) on low heat.

> Remove the outer leaves of the endives. Rinse the endives briefly. Using the sharp point of a knife, gently cut into the bottom and remove a small cone-shaped section of the stalk. Cut the endives in half lengthways. Season with salt and pepper and brush all over with olive oil. Place the endives flat side down on the plancha, and cook for 10–12 minutes, undisturbed. Turn them over, sprinkle with caraway seeds, and brush on some more olive oil. Cook for 8–10 minutes. Remove from the plancha and keep them hot, turning up the heat to maximum.

> Place the salmon noisettes on the plancha and cook for 4–5 minutes. Turn, and cook for another 2 minutes: the salmon should remain slightly pink. Serve immediately with the grilled endives and a drizzle of olive oil.

JOHN DORY SEASONED WITH NUTMEG, AND SWEET POTATO BLINIS

PREPARATION : **45 minutes**
COOKING TIME : **10 minutes**

INGREDIENTS
Serves 6

- 2 lb (900 g) John Dory fillets
- 1¼ lb (600 g) sweet potato
- salt, ground pepper
- 1 clove garlic
- 2 whole nutmegs
- 2 eggs
- ½ sachet (1 tsp) baking powder
- generous 2 tbsp (20 g) all-purpose flour
- 4 tbsp (60 g) fromage frais
- 1 level tsp ground cumin
- a few sprigs chopped cilantro
- 1¼ cups (300 ml) meat gravy or veal stock
- 3½ tbsp (50 g) butter
- 3 tbsp (45 ml) sunflower oil

≫ Peel and wash the sweet potatoes, and cut them into chunks. Cook for 20 minutes in a pan of boiling, salted water with the unpeeled, whole garlic clove.

≫ Grate the two nutmegs onto a large plate.

≫ Cut the John Dory fillets into portions. Dip them in the grated nutmeg on one side only; season with salt and pepper. Put them in the refrigerator.

≫ Drain the sweet potato chunks in a sieve for 10 minutes. Blend them, along with the garlic clove. Add the beaten eggs, flour, baking powder, fromage frais, cumin, and salt and pepper to taste. Combine well until the mixture is a smooth consistency.

≫ In a pan, boil the meat gravy for 10–15 minutes on medium heat to reduce it slightly. Remove from the stovetop, beat in 2 tablespoons of chilled butter, and season with salt and pepper. Keep the gravy warm without boiling.

≫ Melt a knob of butter in a blini pan and then drop in a generous tablespoon of sweet potato batter, spreading it evenly. Cook the blini for 3–4 minutes on each side. Keep it hot. Make the other blinis in the same way (you can use a large frying pan to make 3 or 4 blinis at one time).

≫ Pre-heat and lightly oil the plancha (see p. 4). Grill the John Dory fillets for 3–4 minutes on each side, starting with the nutmeg-coated side. Serve immediately, sprinkled with cilantro, with the blinis and piping hot gravy.

POLLOCK MARINATED IN SWEET CHILI WITH GRILLED CHORIZO

PREPARATION : 15 minutes
MARINADE : 6 hours
COOKING TIME : approx. 15 minutes

INGREDIENTS
Serves 6

- 6 pollock steaks, each approx. 9 oz (250 g)
- 1 small sweet red chili
- 24 thin chorizo slices
- 1 clove garlic
- 1 tsp ground ginger
- 1 tsp caster sugar
- 1 tsp paprika
- salt
- $^2/_3$ cup (150 ml) olive oil

> De-seed and chop the chili. Peel and chop the garlic clove very finely.

> In a bowl containing 3 tablespoons of very hot water, combine the ginger, sugar, paprika, and salt. Whip in the olive oil and then add the chili and garlic.

> Pour half of this marinade into a large dish. Place the pollock steaks in the dish and cover with the rest of the marinade. Cover with plastic wrap and refrigerate for 6 hours.

> Pre-heat the plancha (see p. 4).

> Drain the marinade from the fish, reserving the excess. Grill fish steaks for 6–9 minutes each side, depending on the thickness.

> Three minutes before the end of the cooking time, place the chorizo slices on the plancha and cook for 1–2 minutes each side.

> Place 4 chorizo slices on top of each pollock steak. Drizzle lightly with the chili marinade and serve immediately.

Serve the pollock with saffron-flavored fried rice and grilled bell peppers. Drizzle all over with marinade before serving.

TROUT CROQUETTES WITH WASABI AND COCONUT SAUCE

PREPARATION : 40 minutes
COOKING TIME : 10 minutes

INGREDIENTS

Serves 6

- 1½ lb (700 g) sea trout fillet, skin removed
- 3 shallots
- 1 tbsp wasabi
- 3 tbsp (45 ml) olive oil + a small amount for grilling
- salt, ground pepper
- 1 large onion
- 1¼ cups (300 ml) coconut milk
- $^2/_3$ cup (150 ml) fish stock (see recipe p. 12)
- 2 tbsp ginger paste (available from Asian grocery stores)
- 1 level tbsp curry powder
- 1¼ lb (600 g) mange-touts

≫ Remove the gray flesh and bones from the trout fillet. Chop the flesh finely with a knife. Peel and chop the shallots.

≫ In a mixing bowl, mash together the chopped trout, shallots, wasabi, half of the olive oil, and season with salt and pepper. Shape the mixture into 18 croquettes with your hands, and lay them on a plate. Put them in the refrigerator.

≫ Peel and chop the onion. Sweat the onion in a pan with the remaining olive oil for 5 minutes. Pour in the fish stock, bring to a boil, and reduce it by half. Add the coconut milk, ginger paste, curry powder, and some salt and pepper. Cook for about 15 minutes on low heat.

≫ Meanwhile, wash the mange-touts and pre-cook them for 3 minutes in a large pan of boiling, salted water. Drain, and rinse under cold running water.

≫ Pre-heat and lightly oil the plancha (see p. 4).

≫ Brown the trout croquettes on the plancha for 5–7 minutes, turning frequently. Put the mange-touts on the plancha and cook for another 3 minutes.

≫ Whisk up the coconut sauce and serve it with the trout croquettes and mange-touts.

PREPARATION: **40 minutes**
COOKING TIME: **10 minutes**

GURNARD FILLETS WITH CURRY VINAIGRETTE

INGREDIENTS

Serves 6

- 6 gurnard, each approx. 14 oz (400 g)
- salt, ground pepper
- 1¾ cups (200 g) Parmesan, freshly grated
- 3 cups (250 g) mixed leaf salad
- ¼ cup (60 ml) wine vinegar
- 1 level tbsp Madras curry powder
- 7 tbsp (100 ml) olive oil

≫ Pre-heat the oven to 180 °C (355 °F).

≫ De-scale the gurnard and fillet the flesh, removing the bones. Season the fish with salt and pepper, and refrigerate.

≫ Spread the grated Parmesan on a baking sheet covered in wax paper. Bake in the oven for 8–10 minutes until golden. Leave to cool and break into pieces.

≫ Pre-heat the plancha (see p. 4).

≫ In a pan, heat the vinegar with 3 tablespoons of water. Remove from the stovetop, add the curry powder, and season with salt and pepper. When the curry powder has dissolved, pour in the olive oil. Blend together until you have thick, smooth vinaigrette. Leave it to cool down.

≫ Grill the gurnard fillets for 3–4 minutes on each side, starting with the skin side down. Drizzle with half of the curry-flavored vinaigrette.

≫ Season the mixed salad with the remaining vinaigrette.

≫ Serve the gurnard fillets very hot with Parmesan tuiles and mixed leaf salad.

SPICY MACKEREL WITH BACON

PREPARATION : 30 minutes
COOKING TIME : 10 minutes

INGREDIENTS
Serves 6

- 4 large (or 6 medium size) mackerel
- 20 thin slices smoked bacon
- 1¾ lb (800 g) firm waxy potatoes (fingerling)
- 1 oz (30 g) ground cubeb pepper (or allspice)
- 1 ²/₃ cups (400 ml) heavy cream
- 3 tbsp (45 ml) olive oil
- salt, ground pepper

≫ Trim the mackerel fins, cut off the heads, then without gutting them (to keep the stomach intact) cut them into 18 large slices. Now remove the guts (leaving the portions intact). Rinse well and pat dry with a clean cloth.

≫ Wrap 1 slice of bacon around each portion, and tie firmly with kitchen twine. Lightly brush with oil on the flesh side, dip in the ground cubeb pepper, and season with salt. Put them in the refrigerator.

≫ Wash the potatoes and cook them in a pan of boiling, salted water for 20 minutes.

≫ In a pan, brown the rest of the bacon (chopped up). Add the cream, and season with salt and pepper. Bring to a boil, and cook for 10 minutes until the sauce has thickened slightly. Whizz with a hand blender.

≫ Drain the potatoes and slice them into rounds, but do not peel them. Put them in the pan with the sauce and keep hot.

≫ Pre-heat the plancha (see p. 4).

≫ Grill the mackerel pieces for 4–5 minutes on each side. Serve immediately with the creamy potatoes.

SEA BASS WITH GRILLED SAUSAGE IN CIDER VINEGAR

PREPARATION: 30 minutes
MARINADE: 2 hours
COOKING TIME: 15 minutes

INGREDIENTS
Serves 6

- 3 sea bass, each weighing 1¼–2 lb (800–900 g)
- 1 cup (250 ml) cider vinegar
- 3 tbsp (45 ml) olive oil
- generous 1 tbsp brown sugar
- 500 g smoked sausage (e.g. andouille or Cajun)
- 10 tbsp (140 g) slightly salted butter
- salt, ground pepper

❯ De-scale the fish and cut off the heads. Gut them carefully and cut into slices. Rinse well under cold running water.

❯ In a bowl, combine 3 tablespoons of cider vinegar with salt and pepper, then add the olive oil. Pour half of the mixture into a shallow, flat dish. Place the sea bass steaks in the dish and brush with the rest of the marinade. Cover with plastic wrap and marinate in the refrigerator for 2 hours.

❯ Put the remaining vinegar in a pan with 7 tablespoons of water and the brown sugar, and reduce by half on high heat. Lower the heat and beat in the butter (chilled and diced). Season with salt and pepper. Boil vigorously for 3 minutes. Whizz the sauce with a hand blender. Keep it hot.

❯ Pre-heat the plancha (see p. 4). Remove the sausage skin. Cut into slices 2–2½ inches (5–6 cm) thick, then cut each slice in half.

❯ Drain the sea bass steaks, discarding any excess marinade. Place them on the plancha and cook for 5–6 minutes on one side, then turn them over. At the same time, put the sausage halves on the plancha. Grill everything for another 5–6 minutes, turning the sausage pieces once or twice.

❯ Serve the sea bass steaks and sausage with the cider vinegar sauce, and a side dish of buttered samphire.

SEARED BLUEFIN TUNA WITH CORIANDER TWO-WAYS

INGREDIENTS

Serves 6

- 2¼ lb (1 kg) bluefin tuna
- 1 clove garlic
- 1 bunch fresh cilantro leaves
- generous 1 tbsp coriander seeds
- 1 level tsp ground ginger
- ²/₃ cup (150 ml) olive oil
- 2 large zucchini
- salt, ground pepper

≫ Peel the garlic clove. Wash the cilantro and remove the stalks.

≫ Put the coriander seeds in a food chopper. Add the cilantro leaves, garlic, ginger, olive oil, salt, and pepper. Whizz the mixture for 2 minutes.

≫ Cut the tuna into 6 thick slices.

≫ Pour half of the coriander marinade into a shallow, flat dish. Place the tuna slices in it and pour the rest of the marinade over them. Cover with plastic wrap and refrigerate for 4 hours.

≫ Wash the zucchini and cut them into generous 2-inch- (5–7-cm-) rounds. Season with salt and pepper.

≫ Pre-heat the plancha (see p. 4).

≫ Drain the marinade from the tuna slices, reserving the excess.

≫ Brown the zucchini slices on the plancha for 5 minutes on each side. At the same time, place the tuna on the plancha and cook for 8–10 minutes on one side, and just 1–2 minutes on the other side. The tuna should still be slightly raw in the middle (reduce the cooking time if the slices are thinner).

≫ Brush the tuna and zucchini with marinade and serve.

You can also grill a thinly sliced fennel bulb with the zucchini.

SWORDFISH WITH SPICY WASABI SAUCE

PREPARATION : **30 minutes**
COOKING TIME : **15 minutes**

INGREDIENTS
Serves 6

- 6 swordfish fillets, each approx. 6½ oz (180 g)
- 1 small bunch flat-leaf parsley
- 6 green onions
- 1 small red chili
- 4 cloves garlic
- salt, ground pepper
- juice of 2 lemons
- generous 1 tbsp brown sugar
- 7 tbsp (100 ml) grapeseed or sunflower oil + a small amount for grilling
- generous 1 tsp wasabi

》 To prepare the spicy sauce: wash and chop the parsley. Peel the green onions, keeping 2 inches of green stem, and thinly slice them. De-seed and chop the chili. Peel and chop the garlic cloves.

》 In a bowl, mix together the parsley, chili, garlic, onions with stems, and salt and pepper to taste.

》 Pour the lemon juice into a pan. Add 3 tablespoons of water, the oil, and the brown sugar. Stir and bring to a boil on medium heat. As soon as it boils, turn off the heat, and pour the mixture into the bowl with the other ingredients. Add the wasabi, mix well, and leave to cool.

》 Pre-heat and lightly oil the plancha (see p. 4).

》 Season the swordfish pieces with salt and pepper and then grill them for 6—8 minutes on each side. Serve immediately, coated with the spicy sauce.

As an accompaniment, serve a tomato salad with sherry and balsamic vinaigrette.

Sardines with herb pesto

PREPARATION: **30 minutes**
COOKING TIME: **10 minutes**

INGREDIENTS
Serves 6

- 18 large fresh sardines
- 1¾ lb (750 g) firm waxy potatoes
  (fingerling)
- 4 cloves garlic
- 1 small bunch cilantro
- 1 small bunch chervil
- 1 small bunch tarragon
- 1 small bunch flat-leaf parsley
- 7 tbsp (50 g) grated Parmesan
- 1 oz (30 g) pine nuts
- 2 tbsp (30 g) butter
- salt, ground pepper
- generous ¾ cup (200 ml) olive oil
  + a small amount for grilling

》 Gut the sardines, rinse under cold running water, and drain in a sieve.

》 Wash the potatoes (do not peel), and cook them in a pan of boiling, salted water for 15 minutes. Drain, and rinse under cold water.

》 Peel 1 garlic clove and remove any green shoots.

》 Wash the herbs and remove the stalks. Put the leaves in a food processor with the garlic clove, pine nuts, and Parmesan. Blend well for 2 minutes. Add $^2/_3$ cup (150 ml) olive oil, and some salt and pepper, then blend for another 1 minute until the pesto is nice and smooth. Spoon the pesto into a bowl.

》 Peel and thinly slice the remaining garlic cloves.

》 Cut the potatoes in half lengthways. Put them in a frying pan with the rest of the oil and the butter. Season with salt and pepper and brown for 10–15 minutes, adding the sliced garlic half way through the cooking time.

》 Pre-heat and lightly oil the plancha (see p. 4).

》 Season the sardines with salt and pepper. Grill them for 4–5 minutes on each side.

》 Arrange the sardines on plates and pour over the herb pesto. Spoon the garlicky potatoes on the side and serve immediately.

SESAME SEA BREAM AND TOMATO COMPOTE

PREPARATION : 45 minutes
COOKING TIME : 10 minutes

INGREDIENTS
Serves 6

- 6 sea bream, each approx. 14 oz (400 g)
- 3 tbsp (45 ml) olive oil + a small amount for brushing the fish
- 5 oz (140 g) sesame seeds
- salt, ground pepper
- 6 large tomatoes
- 5 shallots
- generous 1 tbsp brown sugar
- 2 tbsp (10 ml) sherry vinegar
- 3 tbsp (45 ml) balsamic vinegar
- 3 tbsp (45 ml) sesame oil

❯ De-scale and fillet the sea bream, removing the bones (you can ask your fishmonger to do this). Brush the fillets with a little olive oil, and coat the skin sides with 4 ounces of the sesame seeds, pressing down lightly. Season the fillets with salt and pepper and place in the refrigerator.

❯ Plunge the tomatoes in a pan of boiling water for 20 seconds. Drain, and cool them down in cold water. Remove the skins and seeds and then coarsely chop the flesh.

❯ Peel and thinly slice the shallots. Sweat them for 5 minutes in a pan containing 3 tablespoons of olive oil. Add the chopped tomatoes, brown sugar, and some salt and pepper. Cook for 30 minutes on medium heat, stirring frequently.

❯ In a non-stick pan, dry-roast the remaining sesame seeds on low heat for 2 minutes. Leave them to cool.

❯ In a high-sided bowl, mix together the two vinegars with 3 tablespoons of hot water and season with salt and pepper. Add the sesame oil, the remaining olive oil, and the toasted sesame seeds. Whizz this all together for 20 seconds using a hand blender until the vinaigrette is silky smooth.

❯ Pre-heat and lightly oil the plancha (see p. 4).

❯ Place the coated fish on the plancha, skin side down, and brown for 5 minutes. Turn, and brown the other side for 4–5 minutes.

❯ Coat the fish with the sesame dressing and serve with tomato compote.

TURBOT WITH POPPY SEEDS

PREPARATION : **45 minutes**
COOKING TIME : **20 minutes**

INGREDIENTS

Serves 6

- 6 turbot portions, each approx. 14 oz (350–400 g)
- 2 Swiss chard heads
- 2 large shallots, peeled and chopped
- generous 1 tbsp black peppercorns, coarsely ground
- $^2/_3$ cup (150 ml) white wine vinegar
- 7 tbsp (100 ml) olive oil
- 5½ oz (150 g) poppy seeds
- salt, ground pepper

For the béarnaise sauce with basil

- 15 basil leaves, chopped
- 5 egg yolks
- 1 $^1/_3$ cups (300 g) butter

≫ Remove the green leaves from the Swiss chard. Wash the stalks and plunge them whole into a large pan of boiling, salted water for 15 minutes. Drain, and rinse in cold water.

≫ Put the shallots in a pan with the coarsely ground peppercorns and the vinegar. Reduce for 8–10 minutes on medium heat until the liquid is absorbed. Leave to cool.

≫ Season the turbot pieces with salt and pepper, coat them in olive oil, then dip them in the poppy seeds.

≫ For the béarnaise sauce, melt the butter in a double boiler, then clarify by removing the curds on the surface and at the bottom. Put the egg yolks in the pan with the shallot reduction, and add 2 tablespoons of water. Cook on very low heat for 6–8 minutes, beating continuously, to make a light frothy sauce. Remove the pan from the heat, and keep beating for a further 3 minutes to stop the cooking process. Gradually whip in the clarified butter. Season with salt and pepper. Pass the béarnaise sauce through a fine strainer.

≫ Stir the basil leaves into the sauce. Keep at room temperature.

≫ Pre-heat the plancha (see p. 4).

≫ Cut the chard stalks in three lengthways. Brush with olive oil, and season with salt and pepper.

≫ Grill the turbot and chard at the same time: cook the fish for 8–10 minutes on each side, and turn the chard occasionally. Serve with the basil-flavored béarnaise sauce.

Red mullet stuffed with olives and fennel

INGREDIENTS

Serves 6

- 6 red mullet, each 11–14 oz
  (300–400 g)
- 1 medium fennel bulb
- 1 clove garlic
- 3 oz (80 g) black olives, pitted
- 6 basil leaves
- 6 tbsp (50 g) pine nuts
- 1 tbsp black olive tapenade
- 7 tbsp (100 ml) olive oil + a small
  amount for grilling
- salt, ground pepper

》 De-scale and gut the red mullet, then rinse under cold running water. Put them in the refrigerator.

》 Wash and thinly slice the fennel. Peel and chop the garlic clove. Roughly chop the olives. Gently shred the basil.

》 In a frying pan, cook the fennel and garlic in half of the olive oil for 10–15 minutes on low heat. Season with salt and pepper.

》 Add the olives, then the pine nuts and basil. Continue to cook for a further 5 minutes. Leave it to cool.

》 In a bowl, stir the remaining oil into the tapenade. Keep it to one side.

》 Pre-heat and lightly oil the plancha (see p. 4).

》 Carefully stuff the fish with the fennel mixture. Tie them closed with kitchen twine, then season with salt and pepper.

》 Grill the red mullet for 5–6 minutes on each side. Serve immediately, coated with the tapenade oil.

Serve the red mullet with a Provençal vegetable tian.

GRILLED COD WITH FIERY SAUCE AND GARLIC PURÉE

PREPARATION: 40 minutes
COOKING TIME: 15 minutes

INGREDIENTS
Serves 6

- 6 salt-cod steaks (pre-soaked to remove salt), each approx. 5½ oz (160 g)
- 1 onion
- 1½ oz (40 g) fresh ginger
- 1 small red chili
- 7 tbsp (100 ml) grapeseed or sunflower oil + a small amount for grilling
- 1 tsp caster sugar
- 2 tbsp nuoc-mam (fish sauce)
- 3 tbsp (45 ml) white wine vinegar
- juice of 2 lemons
- salt, ground pepper
- 2 lb (900 g) red potatoes
- 4 cloves garlic
- generous ¾ cup (200 ml) milk
- 4 tbsp (60 g) butter
- 2 tbsp thick crème fraîche

≫ To make the hot sauce: peel and chop the onion. Peel and grate the ginger. De-seed and chop the chili.

≫ Heat 2 tablespoons of the oil in a pan, and sweat the onion for 5 minutes. Add the sugar, ginger, fish sauce, vinegar, lemon juice, and salt. Bring to a boil. Pour in the rest of the oil and heat the mixture for 3 minutes. Turn off the heat, add the chili and mix well. Leave it to cool.

≫ Peel and wash the potatoes, then cut them into chunks. Cook for 20 minutes in a pan of boiling, salted water.

≫ Peel the garlic cloves and plunge them in a small pan of boiling water for 5 minutes, then drain. Heat the milk in a pan.

≫ Drain the potatoes and squeeze them through a potato ricer along with the garlic cloves. Add the butter (chopped), the hot milk, crème fraîche, and salt and pepper to taste. Combine it all into a smooth, creamy purée. Keep it hot in a double boiler.

≫ Pre-heat and lightly oil the plancha (see p. 4).

≫ Place the cod steaks on the plancha and brown for 6–7 minutes on each side. Serve piping hot, coated in fiery sauce, with the potato purée on the side.

CURRIED RED MULLET WITH GRILLED BROAD BEANS

PREPARATION : **45 minutes**
MARINADE : **4 hours**
COOKING TIME : **5 minutes**

INGREDIENTS

Serves 6

- 6 large red mullet
- 6½ lb (3 kg) fresh broad beans
- 1 clove garlic
- 1 oz (30 g) ginger root
- 1 level tbsp curry powder
- 2 tbsp (30 ml) lemon juice
- ²/₃ cup (150 ml) olive oil
- salt, ground pepper

≫ De-scale and carefully fillet the red mullet, removing the bones (ideally, ask your fish retailer to do this).

≫ Peel the garlic clove and mash it well with the flat side of a knife. Peel and grate the ginger.

≫ In a bowl, mix together the lemon juice, curry powder, and salt and pepper. Add the garlic and ginger, then half of the olive oil.

≫ Pour half of this marinade into a shallow, flat dish. Place the fillets, skin side down, in the dish. Coat the fillets with the rest of the marinade. Cover with plastic wrap and refrigerate for 4 hours.

≫ Meanwhile, shell the broad beans and cook for 5 minutes in a pan of boiling, salted water. Drain and rinse in cold water. Carefully remove the skins.

≫ Pre-heat the plancha (see p. 4).

≫ In a bowl, mix the broad beans with the rest of the olive oil, and season with salt and pepper. Drain the marinade off the fillets.

≫ Place the beans on one corner of the plancha and cook for 5 minutes, stirring occasionally. At the same time, brown the fish fillets on the plancha for 2–3 minutes each side. Serve immediately.

PREPARATION: **45 minutes**
COOKING TIME: **20 minutes**

SALMON PATTIES WITH BACON AND ONION

INGREDIENTS
Serves 6

- 1¾ lb (800 g) premium quality Scottish salmon fillet, skin removed
- 1 large red onion, peeled and chopped
- ¹/₃ cup (80 ml) olive oil + a small amount for grilling
- 1 tbsp liquid honey
- 1 tsp ground cumin
- 2 pinches cinnamon
- 9 large bacon slices, finely chopped
- 3 sprigs flat-leaf parsley
- salt, ground pepper
- 1 large piece sausage casing (from your butcher)

≫ In a frying pan, sweat the onion in 3 tablespoons of olive oil on medium heat for 6–8 minutes. Add the honey, cumin, and cinnamon, and lightly caramelize. Mix in the bacon bits and continue to cook for 3–4 minutes on medium heat, stirring the mixture. Leave to cool.

≫ Remove the gray flesh and bones from the salmon fillet. Finely chop the flesh with a knife. Wash and chop the parsley.

≫ Combine the chopped salmon and parsley in a bowl. Add the caramelized onion and bacon; season with salt and pepper.

≫ Cut the sausage casing into squares of approximately 6 x 6 inches (15 x 15 cm).

≫ Shape the salmon mixture into 12 balls. Place 1 ball in the middle of each casing square, then fold it closed tightly. Gently flatten the patties with the palm of your hand.

≫ Pre-heat and lightly oil the plancha (see p. 4).

≫ Brush the patties with the remaining olive oil. Grill for 6–8 minutes on each side. Serve immediately with a mixed leaf salad.

GRILLED HERRING AND BLUE POTATOES WITH MUSTARD

PREPARATION : 30 minutes
COOKING TIME : 10 minutes

INGREDIENTS

Serves 6

- 12 fresh herring
- 3 tbsp (45 ml) olive oil
- 3 oz (80 g) mustard seeds
- salt, ground pepper
- 1¾ lb (800 g) blue/purple potatoes
- ²/₃ cup (150 ml) fish stock (see recipe p. 12)
- 1 ²/₃ cups (400 ml) heavy cream
- generous 2 tbsp strong mustard

≫ Gut and rinse the herring under cold running water. Brush with olive oil and place them in a dish. Sprinkle both sides with mustard seeds, and season with salt and pepper. Put the dish in the refrigerator.

≫ Peel and wash the potatoes. Cook for 20 minutes in a pan of boiling, salted water.

≫ Meanwhile, pour the fish stock into a pan and boil for 5 minutes. Add the cream, and season with salt and pepper. Boil for 8—10 minutes on medium heat until the sauce thickens slightly. Stir in the mustard. Keep the sauce hot, but do not boil.

≫ Pre-heat the plancha (see p. 4).

≫ Drain the potatoes and rinse under cold water. Cut them in half.

≫ Place the potatoes on one side of the plancha, and brown for 8—10 minutes. At the same time cook the herring on the other side of the plancha for 4—5 minutes on each side.

≫ Transfer the herring and potatoes to the plates. Pour on the mustard sauce and serve immediately.

MONKFISH WITH GRILLED LEEKS AND RED ONIONS

PREPARATION: 30 minutes
COOKING TIME: 30 minutes

INGREDIENTS
Serves 6

- 2 lb (900 g) monkfish fillet
- 12 baby (or 6 medium) leeks
- ½–⅔ cup (120–150 ml) olive oil
- salt, ground pepper
- 1 small bunch cilantro
- 1 level tsp coriander seeds
- 3 tbsp lemon juice
- ¼ tsp (1 g) harissa
- 3 red onions

》 Cut the monkfish fillet into 18 slices, each approximately ⅓ inch (1 cm) thick. Season with salt and pepper and put in the refrigerator.

》 Wash the leeks and remove any coarse green parts; cut them in half lengthways.

》 Pre-heat the plancha (see p. 4) on a low heat.

》 Brush the leeks lightly with oil and place them on the plancha. Cook for 20–25 minutes, turning frequently and basting lightly with olive oil as they cook. Season with salt and pepper.

》 Meanwhile, wash the cilantro and remove the stalks. Combine the lemon juice in a high-sided bowl with salt and pepper, the coriander seeds, harissa, half of the cilantro leaves, and 7 tablespoons of olive oil. Mix thoroughly using a hand blender until the vinaigrette is smooth and creamy.

》 Peel and thinly slice the onions. Chop the remaining cilantro leaves. In a bowl, combine half of the lemon vinaigrette with the coriander and sliced onion.

》 When the leeks are nice and tender, remove them from the plancha and increase to full heat.

》 Grill the monkfish portions for 3–4 minutes on each side.

》 Arrange the leeks and the onion salad on plates. Put 3 pieces of monkfish on each plate. Drizzle with the rest of the lemon vinaigrette and serve immediately.

Seared scallops with preserved lemon

PREPARATION : 30 minutes
COOKING TIME : 5 minutes

INGREDIENTS
Serves 6

- 30 fresh scallops, coral removed
- 1¼ lb (600 g) baby spinach
- ½ preserved lemon
- 2 sprigs cilantro
- ⅓ cup (80 ml) rice vinegar
- generous 1 tbsp liquid honey
- salt, ground pepper
- 7 tbsp (100 ml) olive oil + a small
  amount for grilling
- 3 tbsp orange juice

≫ Wash and drain the baby spinach. Remove the seeds from the preserved lemon and dice it finely. Remove the cilantro stalks and chop the leaves.

≫ In a pan, heat the rice vinegar with the honey, salt, and pepper. Remove from heat and add the olive oil, chopped lemon and cilantro, and the orange juice. Whizz with a hand blender until the dressing is silky smooth.

≫ Pre-heat and lightly oil the plancha (see p. 4).

≫ Season the scallops with salt and pepper and grill for 2–3 minutes on each side. Remove from the plancha and keep them hot.

≫ Put the baby spinach on the very hot plancha. Season and cook for 2 minutes, stirring continuously.

≫ Divide the spinach between the serving plates. Place 5 seared scallops on top and drizzle all over with the preserved lemon dressing.

OYSTER SKEWERS WITH LEMONGRASS

PREPARATION : **45 minutes**
MARINADE : **6 hours**
COOKING TIME : **10 minutes**

INGREDIENTS
Serves 6

- 30 medium size oysters
  (approx. 2 oz/60 g each)
- 1 small red chili
- 2 lemongrass stalks
- 3 sprigs cilantro
- 1 onion
- 7 tbsp (100 ml) olive oil
- salt, ground pepper
- 2 eggs
- 9 tbsp (80 g) all-purpose flour
- 7 oz (200 g) panko or traditional
  breadcrumbs
- 2 tbsp fish sauce
- 3 tbsp sweet soy sauce
- generous 1 tbsp (20 g) caster
  sugar
- 3 tbsp sunflower or grapeseed oil
  for grilling

≫ Prise open the oysters over a pan and carefully detach the flesh from the shell. Put the flesh in the pan and heat it up. Turn off the heat as soon as the oysters begin to simmer and leave to cook in their juices. Drain on paper towels and put them in a shallow, flat dish.

≫ De-seed and chop the chili. Remove the outer leaves of the lemongrass and finely slice the tenderest part. Wash and chop the cilantro. Peel and chop the onion.

≫ In a pan, gently sweat the onion in 2 tablespoons of olive oil for 5 minutes. Add the chili and lemongrass, salt, and pepper. Cook for a further 2 minutes. Add the soy sauce, fish sauce, sugar, remaining olive oil, and cilantro. Heat the mixture for 2 minutes. Turn off the heat and leave to cool.

≫ Pour the marinade over the oysters. Cover with plastic wrap and refrigerate for 6 hours.

≫ Beat the eggs in a shallow, flat dish. Put the flour and breadcrumbs onto 2 separate plates.

≫ Drain the marinade off the oysters (reserving it), and dip them in turn into the flour, beaten egg, and then the crumbs. Insert a wooden skewer through each oyster.

≫ Pre-heat the plancha (see p. 4), and oil it liberally with the sunflower or grapeseed oil.

≫ Grill the oyster skewers on each side for 3–5 minutes, and serve immediately (with the marinade on the side, if you like).

SCOLLOP SKEWERS WITH SHIITAKE MUSHROOMS

PREPARATION : 40 minutes
COOKING TIME : 10 minutes

INGREDIENTS
Serves 6

- 24 large scallops
- 14 oz (400 g) shiitake mushrooms
- 2½ oz (75 g) breadcrumbs
- 3½ oz (100 g) hazelnuts
- ¾ oz (20 g) peanuts
- 2 pinches hot chili powder
- 1 level tbsp caster sugar
- 3 tbsp olive oil
- salt, ground pepper

》 Rinse the mushrooms briefly under cold running water and then drain on paper towels. Cut any large ones in half.

》 In a food chopper, combine the hazelnuts, peanuts, sugar, chili, 1 tablespoon of olive oil, and the breadcrumbs. Whizz the mixture for 2 minutes until you have fine, nutty breadcrumbs.

》 Pre-heat and liberally oil the plancha (see p. 4).

》 Put the mushrooms on the plancha and cook for 4–5 minutes, stirring frequently. Season with salt and pepper. Remove them from the plancha and leave to cool.

》 On each skewer, thread 4 scallops and mushrooms alternately. Season the skewers with salt and pepper.

》 Oil the plancha liberally again and cook the scallop skewers for 2–3 minutes on one side. Turn them over, sprinkle with the nutty crumbs, and brown for 2 minutes.

》 Take the skewers off the plancha and cook the nut crumbs for a further 2 minutes, stirring with a spatula until they have caramelized slightly.

》 Sprinkle the skewers with nut crumbs and serve immediately. Serve with spaghetti or linguine with sesame seeds and wasabi.

Crispy grilled clams with ginger

PREPARATION: 30 minutes
COOKING TIME: 10 minutes

INGREDIENTS
Serves 6

- 8¾ lb (4 kg) clams
- 2 onions
- 1 celery stick
- 7 tbsp (100 ml) olive oil
- ²/₃ cup (150 ml) white wine
- salt, ground pepper
- 2½ oz (70 g) ginger
- 3 cloves garlic
- 1 bunch cilantro
- 3 oz (80 g) breadcrumbs
- 3 tbsp sweet soy sauce

》 Wash the clams thoroughly, changing the water several times. Drain in a sieve.

》 Peel and chop 1 onion. Trim the celery and dice it finely.

》 In a large frying pan, sweat the chopped onion and celery with one third of the olive oil on medium heat for 5 minutes. Add the clams, white wine, and pepper. Cover the pan and cook on high heat for 10 minutes, stirring the clams around half way through the cooking time. Leave to cool, then remove the shells.

》 Peel and chop the other onion and the garlic cloves. Wash and chop the cilantro. Peel and finely slice the ginger.

》 Pre-heat the plancha. Pour one third of the oil into the pan and gently brown the chopped onion and garlic with some salt and pepper for 5 minutes, stirring with a metal spoon. Add the ginger and cook for another 5 minutes.

》 Place the clams on the plancha. Add the breadcrumbs, cilantro, and the rest of the oil. Brown for 5 minutes, mixing all the time to coat the clams in the breadcrumbs and garnish.

》 Drizzle the soy sauce over the clams. Remove immediately from the plancha and eat right away.

Serve the clams with fried spaghetti, seasoned with soy sauce.

MUSSELS WITH SWEET POTATO FRIES

PREPARATION: **40 minutes**
COOKING TIME: **30 minutes**

INGREDIENTS
Serves 6

- 11 lb (5 kg) fresh mussels
- 1 onion
- 1 celery stick
- 2 tbsp (30 g) butter
- ¾ lb (350 g) smoked bacon
- 1 bouquet garni
- generous ¾ cup (200 ml) white wine
- salt, ground pepper
- 2¼ lb (1 kg) sweet potatoes
- 7 tbsp (100 ml) olive oil + a small amount for grilling
- 1 bunch parsley

》 Scrub the mussels and wash them thoroughly, changing the water several times. Drain them in a sieve.

》 Peel and chop the onion. Trim the celery and dice it very finely.

》 In a large fying pan, sweat the onion and celery in the butter for 3 minutes on medium heat. Add the mussels, white wine, bouquet garni, and pepper. Cover the pan and cook for approximately 10 minutes on high heat, shaking the pan occasionally to ensure even cooking. Leave them to cool and remove the shells.

》 Peel and wash the sweet potatoes; cut them into small fries.

》 Pre-heat the plancha (see p. 4) on medium heat and then coat with olive oil.

》 Place the sweet potato fries flat down on the plancha. Season with salt and pepper. Cook them for 15–20 minutes, turning every 5 minutes and brushing with olive oil.

》 Meanwhile, finely dice the bacon or cut it into thin strips. Wash and chop the parsley.

》 Take the fries off the plancha and keep them hot. Turn up the heat and brown the bacon bits for 6–8 minutes.

》 Put the mussels and parsley on the plancha and season with salt and pepper. Mix well and brown for a few minutes. Serve immediately with the sweet potato fries.

SHELLFISH PARCELS

PREPARATION : 30 minutes
COOKING TIME : 10 minutes

INGREDIENTS
Serves 6

For the mussel and herb parcels
- 5½ lb (2½ kg) mussels, washed thoroughly and drained
- 1 onion, peeled and chopped
- 2 shallots, peeled and chopped
- 1 celery stick, trimmed and finely diced
- 7 tbsp (100 ml) olive oil
- generous ¾ cup (200 ml) white wine
- 3 sprigs thyme
- 1 large sprig rosemary
- 1 bunch chives, chopped
- 3 sprigs chervil, chopped
- 3 tbsp olive oil
- salt, ground pepper

For the citrus cockle parcels
- 6¾ lb (3 kg) cockles, washed thoroughly and drained
- 3 oranges
- 4 shallots, peeled and chopped
- 7 tbsp (100 ml) white wine
- ⅔ cup (150 ml) heavy cream
- ⅔ cup (150 g) butter
- juice of ½ lemon
- salt, ground pepper
- ⅔ cup (150 g) butter
- 4 sprigs thyme

》 To make the mussel and herb parcels: in a pan, sweat the onion, shallots, and celery in the olive oil for 5 minutes on medium heat. Add the white wine, rosemary and thyme sprigs, and salt and pepper. Boil for 5 minutes on medium heat.

》 Pre-heat the plancha (see p. 4). Cut out 6 large squares of aluminum foil or waxed paper. Divide the mussels between the squares, placing them in the center. Pour on a small amount of the white wine mixture. Sprinkle with chervil and chives. Carefully close the parcels.

》 Place the parcels on the very hot plancha and cook, undisturbed, for 10 minutes. Serve immediately.

》 To make the citrus cockle parcels: zest 2 of the oranges and squeeze the juice from all three.

》 Put one quarter of the shallots and one quarter of the zest in a pan. Add the white wine and reduce by two-thirds on medium heat. Pour in the cream and one third of the orange juice, then boil for another 6–8 minutes on medium heat. Remove from the stovetop and beat in the cold, diced butter. Season with salt and pepper and then add the lemon juice. Keep it hot.

》 Pre-heat the plancha to maximum. In a bowl, mix the remaining orange juice with the thyme, olive oil, remaining shallots, orange zest, and salt and pepper to taste. Cut out 6 large squares of aluminum foil or waxed paper. Divide the cockles between them, placing them in the center of each square, then pour on a small amount of the orange mixture. Close the parcels and place them on the plancha. Cook, undisturbed, for approximately 10 minutes. Serve immediately with the citrus butter.

GRILLED WHELKS IN AIOLI

PREPARATION: 1 hour
SOAKING TIME: 1 hour
COOKING TIME: 15 minutes

INGREDIENTS

Serves 6

- 7¾ lb (3½ kg) live whelks, soaked for 1 hour in a bowl of cold water containing a handful of salt
- 2 tbsp Espelette pepper
- coarse sea salt
- 1 bay leaf
- 2 sprigs thyme
- 3 large carrots, peeled
- 2 large zucchini
- 12 red potatoes
- 3 cloves garlic, peeled and green shoots removed
- generous 1 tbsp (18 g) mustard
- 1 egg yolk
- 3 tbsp (45 ml) sunflower oil
- ⅔ cup (150 ml) olive oil + a small amount for grilling
- salt, ground pepper
- 18 cherry tomatoes
- 6 hard-boiled eggs

≫ Rinse the whelks in several changes of cold water and drain them. Put them in a pan with 1 tablespoon of Espelette pepper, 1 handful of coarse sea salt, and the thyme and bay leaf. Cover well with cold water. Bring to a boil and cook for 30 minutes on medium heat, skimming the surface frequently.

≫ Cut the carrots and zucchini into fairly thick rounds. Cook the potatoes for 20 minutes in a pan of boiling, salted water. In another pan, boil the carrots for 12–15 minutes and the zucchini for 5 minutes. Drain and rinse all the vegetables under cold water. Set them to one side.

≫ To make the aioli, crush the garlic to a paste in a bowl, using a pestle. Combine it with the mustard and egg yolk. Gradually pour in the sunflower oil and 7 tablespoons of olive oil, beating all the time as you would for mayonnaise. Season with salt and pepper.

≫ Drain the whelks, rinse under cold water, and remove the shells. Make sure you remove the small operculum (thin hard covering at the opening of the shell) and the dark back end of the intestine.

≫ Pre-heat and oil the plancha. Cut the potatoes in half lengthways. Put the carrots, zucchini, and potatoes on the plancha and cook for 6–8 minutes. Arrange them together on one side of the plancha.

≫ Put the whelks and cherry tomatoes on the plancha and brown for 5 minutes. Drizzle everything with the remaining olive oil and sprinkle with Espelette pepper. Serve the whelks and vegetables piping hot with the hard-boiled eggs and aioli.

Catalan-style grilled mussels

PREPARATION : **45 minutes**
COOKING TIME : **15 minutes**

INGREDIENTS

Serves 6

- 8¾ lb (4 kg) mussels
- 3 onions
- 5½ oz (150 g) spicy chorizo
- 4 bell peppers: 2 red, 1 green, 1 yellow
- 3 cloves garlic
- 1 bunch flat-leaf parsley
- 2 sprigs thyme
- 1 level tbsp Espelette pepper
- ⅔ cup (150 ml) white wine
- 2½ tbsp (40 g) butter
- 3 tbsp olive oil
- salt, ground pepper

》 Scrub the mussels and wash them thoroughly, changing the water several times. Drain in a sieve.

》 Peel and chop 1 onion. Sweat the chopped onion in the butter in a large frying pan for 5 minutes on medium heat. Add the mussels, white wine, thyme, and ground pepper. Cover the pan and cook for 10 minutes on high heat, stirring the mussels half way through the cooking time. Turn off the heat and leave them to cool. Remove the shells.

》 Peel the bell peppers and cut them into thin strips. Peel and finely slice the remaining onions and garlic. Wash and chop the parsley.

》 Remove the chorizo skin. Cut it in half lengthways, and then into 1-inch- (3-cm-) slices.

》 Pre-heat the plancha to medium heat. Pour on half of the olive oil, then place the onions and peppers on the plancha; add some salt, and cook for 10 minutes, stirring frequently. Increase the heat to maximum, and add the chorizo slices, garlic, remaining oil, Espelette pepper, and mussels. Cook for 5 minutes, stirring it all together frequently.

》 Check and adjust the seasoning. Sprinkle with chopped parsley and serve immediately.

These mussels can be served as an aperitif, or as a main course with zucchini gratin flavored with caraway seeds.

RAZOR CLAMS WITH ANISEED BUTTER

PREPARATION : **20 minutes**
REFRIGERATION : **20 minutes**
COOKING TIME : **10 minutes**

INGREDIENTS

Serves 6

- 6¾ lb (3 kg) razor clams
- 4 shallots
- 2 cloves garlic
- 1 large bunch chervil
- ²/₃ cup (160 g) butter, softened
- 2 tbsp fennel seeds
- 3 tbsp pastis
- oil for the plancha
- salt, ground pepper

≫ Soak the razor clams in cold, salted water. Rinse several times and drain in a sieve.

≫ Peel and finely chop the shallots and garlic. Wash the chervil and remove the leaves.

≫ Put the butter in a food processor. Add the chervil, fennel seeds, pastis, shallots, and chopped garlic. Blend for 2 minutes.

≫ Transfer the aniseed butter to a bowl and refrigerate for 20 minutes.

≫ Pre-heat and lightly oil the plancha (see p. 4).

≫ Put the aniseed butter in a pan and melt it gently over a very low heat.

≫ Place the razor clams on the very hot plancha and sprinkle with salt and pepper. Cook for 6–8 minutes.

≫ When the razor clams have opened and cooked, carefully coat the insides with a small amount of aniseed butter. Continue to cook for 2 minutes and serve immediately with Provençal tomatoes or zucchini and tomato tian.

SHRIMP SKEWERS WITH PANCETTA AND PARMESAN

PREPARATION : 30 minutes
REFRIGERATION : 1 hour
COOKING TIME : 10 minutes

INGREDIENTS

Serves 6

- 36 medium size shrimp
- 4 oz (120 g) Parmesan
- 1 tsp Espelette pepper
- salt
- 18 thin slices pancetta
- 3 tbsp olive oil
- generous ¾ cup (200 ml) balsamic vinegar
- 1 tbsp caster sugar

≫ Shell the shrimp, retaining the tail end. Carefully cut along the backs and remove the black vein.

≫ Using a vegetable peeler, make thin Parmesan shavings.

≫ Season the shrimp with Espelette pepper and salt, then add some Parmesan shavings.

≫ Place 2 shrimp on each slice of pancetta and roll them up. Thread 3 shrimp rolls tightly onto a skewer. Place the shrimp skewers in a flat dish and drizzle with olive oil. Refrigerate for 1 hour.

≫ Meanwhile, reduce the vinegar in a pan with the sugar and 1 pinch of salt until slightly syrupy. Leave to cool.

≫ Pre-heat the plancha (see p. 4).

≫ Grill the shrimp skewers for 4—5 minutes on each side.

≫ Arrange 3 skewers on each plate and drizzle with the balsamic reduction. Serve immediately with red cabbage salad.

OCTOPUS WITH SAUCE VIERGE AND CILANTRO

PREPARATION : **45 minutes**
REFRIGERATION : **2 hours**
COOKING TIME : **30 minutes**

INGREDIENTS

Serves 6

- 3¼ lb (1½ kg) fresh baby octopus
- 2 red tomatoes
- 2 yellow tomatoes
- 2 green tomatoes
- 4 large shallots
- 1 small bunch cilantro
- salt, ground pepper
- generous ¾ cup (200 ml) olive oil
  + a small amount for grilling

》 Clean the octopus well, ensuring the membranes are removed. Separate the tentacles from the bodies. Rinse everything in clean water and drain in a sieve.

》 Plunge the tomatoes in a pan of boiling water for 20 seconds. Rinse in cold water and drain. Peel the tomatoes, cut them into quarters, remove the seeds, and finely dice the flesh.

》 Peel and chop the shallots. Wash and shred the cilantro.

》 In a bowl, mix the chopped tomatoes with the shallots and cilantro. Season with salt and pepper and add the olive oil. Chill the sauce vierge in the refrigerator for 2 hours.

》 Pre-heat and lightly oil the plancha (see p. 4).

》 Season the octopus with salt and pepper. Place the tentacles on the plancha and cook for 10—15 minutes. Push them over to one side of the plancha so they continue to cook. At the same time, place the octopus bodies on the plancha and cook for 10—15 minutes.

》 Pour one third of the sauce vierge over all of the octopus pieces and grill for another 3 minutes.

》 Pour the remaining sauce into a shallow dish and add the grilled octopus, coating them well. Serve immediately.

Serve the octopus with a little gem lettuce and raisin salad, seasoned with citrus dressing.

JAMAICAN-STYLE CRAYFISH

PREPARATION : **20 minutes**
MARINADE : **2 hours**
COOKING TIME : **20 minutes**

INGREDIENTS

Serves 6

- 6 crayfish tails (shell on)
  weighing 11—14 oz (300—400 g),
  or 3 large ones
- 2 tbsp Jamaican black pepper
- 3 limes
- ½ small red chili
- ²⁄₃ cup (150 g) butter
- 1 level tsp sea salt
- oil for grilling

》 Cut the crayfish tails in half lengthways and put them in a large shallow dish.

》 Grind the pepper. Grate the zest of 2 limes and squeeze the juice out of all three. In a bowl, mix half of the juice and zest with half of the ground pepper.

》 Lightly coat the crayfish flesh with the marinade. Cover in plastic wrap and refrigerate for 2 hours.

》 De-seed and chop the chili. Melt the butter in a pan on low heat. Remove from the stovetop, add the chopped chili, sea salt, and the rest of the lime juice and zest. Mix well, and keep at room temperature.

》 Pre-heat and lightly oil the plancha (see p. 4).

》 Place the crayfish tails, flesh side down, on the plancha and cook for 8—10 minutes. Turn them over, making sure you keep them flat. Coat them with a little of the lime butter, and grill on the shell side for 6—8 minutes, brushing with the butter as they cook to soak the flesh thoroughly. Serve immediately.

The crayfish can be served with grilled lime halves, fragrant rice, crudités with dressing, or carrot and coriander purée.

NORTH AFRICAN-STYLE JUMBO LANGOUSTINES

PREPARATION: **40 minutes**
COOKING TIME: **5 minutes**

INGREDIENTS

Serves 6

- 12 jumbo langoustines
- 4 tomatoes
- 1 medium onion
- 3 cloves garlic
- 1 small bunch fresh cilantro
- 1 preserved lemon quarter
- 1/3 cup (80 ml) olive oil + a small
  amount for grilling
- 1 level tbsp chili powder
- 1 level tbsp ground cumin
- salt, ground pepper
- 3 tbsp (45 ml) lemon juice
- generous 1 tsp caster sugar
- 4 mint leaves

≫ Blanch the tomatoes in boiling water for 20 seconds. Rinse in cold water and drain. Remove the skins, cut them in half, remove the seeds, and chop them.

≫ Peel and chop the onion and garlic. Wash the cilantro and remove the stalks. Dice the preserved lemon quarter finely.

≫ In a frying pan, sweat the onion and garlic in 3 tablespoons of olive oil on medium heat for 5 minutes. Add the diced lemon, spices, chopped tomatoes, lemon juice, sugar, ½ glass (125 ml) of water, and salt and pepper. Cook for 10–15 minutes on low heat, stirring occasionally. Remove from the stovetop and then add the cilantro and mint.

≫ Cut the langoustines in half lengthways and de-vein them. Crush the claws slightly. Season with salt and pepper, and coat in oil.

≫ Pre-heat and lightly oil the plancha (see p. 4).

≫ Place the langoustines, flesh side down, on the plancha and cook for 3 minutes. Turn the langoustines and then cover with the tomato mixture. Cook for another 2–3 minutes. Serve immediately.

Serve the langoustines with piperade or grilled bell peppers marinated in garlic.

CRAB CAKES WiTH GARLiC AND CHiLi

PREPARATION : 30 minutes
COOKING TIME : 5 minutes

INGREDIENTS
Serves 6

- 11 oz (300 g) crab meat
- 14 oz (400 g) pollock or whiting
  fillet, boneless
- 2 shallots
- 2 cloves garlic
- ½ red chili
- salt
- generous 1 tbsp (10 g) pink
  peppercorns
- 3 sprigs flat-leaf parsley
- 7 tbsp (100 ml) olive oil + a small
  amount for grilling

For the sauce
- ¼ red chili
- 1 clove garlic
- 3 tbsp (45 ml) lemon juice
- 7 tbsp (100 ml) olive oil
- 1 level tbsp (12 g) caster sugar
- salt

》 To make the crab cakes: cut the fish fillet into small chunks. Peel and chop the shallots and garlic. Wash and chop the parsley. De-seed and chop the chili.

》 In a food processor, combine the fish pieces with some salt and the pink peppercorns. Add the crab meat, olive oil, shallots, garlic, chili, and parsley. Whizz the mixture for 1 minute until it is like smooth dough.

》 Shape the dough into patties the size of a large walnut and flatten them slightly. Put them on a plate and chill them in the refrigerator.

》 To make the sauce: peel and chop the garlic clove. Peel and chop the chili. In a high-sided bowl, dissolve the sugar with 3 tablespoons of very hot water. Add the garlic, chili, and the remaining ingredients. Whizz for 30 seconds with a hand blender.

》 Pre-heat and lightly oil the plancha (see p. 4).

》 Grill the crab cakes for 5–6 minutes on each side. Serve immediately with the sauce.

FRESH SHRIMP IN PARSLEY SATAY

PREPARATION: **20 minutes**
COOKING TIME: **10 minutes**

INGREDIENTS

Serves 6

- 1¼–1½ lb (600–700 g) fresh raw shrimp
- 2 shallots
- 1 small bunch flat-leaf parsley
- 7 tbsp (100 g) softened butter
- 4 tbsp (60 g) satay sauce (available from Asian delicatessens)
- olive oil for grilling
- salt, ground pepper

》 Peel and chop the shallots very finely. Wash and chop the parsley.

》 In a bowl, combine the butter with the shallots, parsley, satay sauce, and some salt.

》 Pre-heat and lightly oil the plancha (see p. 4).

》 Cook the shrimp on a very hot grill for 5–6 minutes, stirring them with a spatula. Season with salt and pepper.

》 Turn off the heat under the plancha and spread the parsley butter over the cooked shrimp. Keep turning them over for 4–5 minutes so that they continue to cook, coated in the melted butter.

》 Spoon the shrimp onto a dish. Lightly scrape the parsley butter off the plancha and spread it on the shrimp. Serve immediately.

If you are unable to source the satay, grind 2 ounces (60 g) peanuts together with 1 level tablespoon mild chili powder, 1 garlic clove, and a little olive oil.

LOBSTER WITH LIME

INGREDIENTS

Serves 6

- 3 Maine lobster, each weighing
  1½–1¾ lb (700–800 g)
- 2 limes
- 2 shallots
- 9 tbsp (130 g) seaweed butter,
  softened
- salt, ground pepper
- oil for grilling

≫ Wash and zest 1 lime. Squeeze the juice from both limes.

≫ Peel and finely chop the shallots.

≫ In a large bowl, mix the seaweed butter, chopped shallots, lime juice and zest, and some salt and pepper.

≫ Cut the raw lobsters in half, remove the black veins, and break off the claws with a heavy knife. Season the lobsters with salt and pepper.

≫ Pre-heat and lightly oil the plancha (see p. 4).

≫ Put the claws on the plancha and cook for 8–10 minutes, turning half way through the cooking time. Push them to one side of the plancha and leave them to finish cooking, turning frequently. At the same time, place the lobster bodies on the plancha, flesh side down, and cook for 8–10 minutes.

≫ Turn over the lobsters. Spread the lime butter over the heads and flesh. Leave them to cook for another 7–10 minutes, allowing the butter to soak through. Serve immediately with grilled vegetables or vegetable tian.

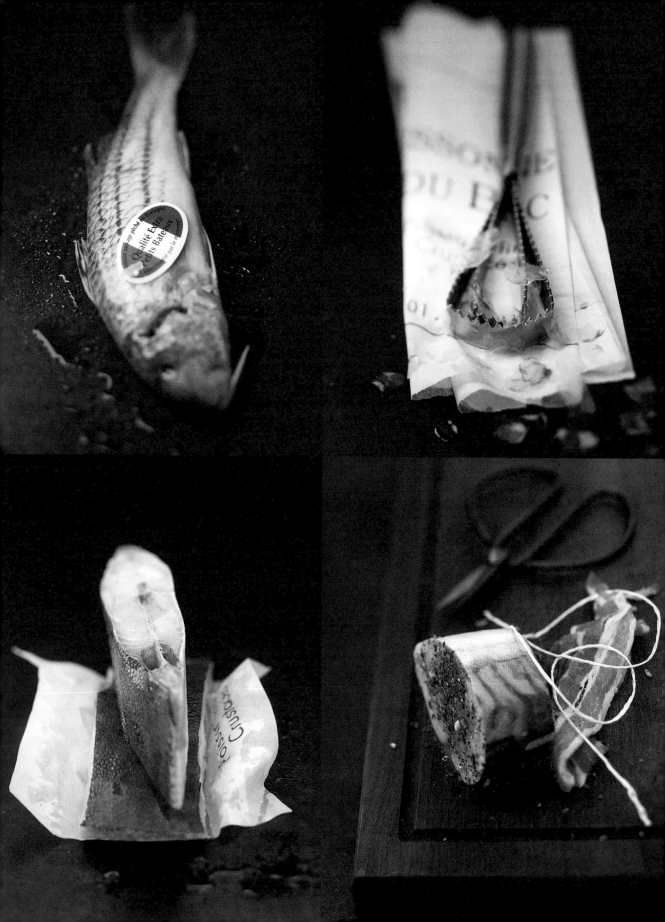

OVEN-BAKED

SKATE TAGINE WITH SAFFRON, APPLES, ALMONDS, AND PUMPKIN

PREPARATION: **45 minutes**
COOKING TIME: **20 minutes**

INGREDIENTS

Serves 6

- 4½ lb (2 kg) thick skate wings
- 3 onions
- 1 carrot
- 1 bouquet garni
- 2 sprigs rosemary
- salt, ground pepper
- 1¾ lb (800 g) pumpkin
- 2 red apples
- 1 clove garlic
- ²/₃ cup (150 ml) olive oil
- generous 3 pinches saffron
- generous 2 tbsp liquid honey
- 4 oz (120 g) whole almonds

≫ In a large pot, bring plenty of water to a boil with 1 sliced onion, the carrot (peeled and sliced into rounds), the bouquet garni, rosemary, and salt and pepper. Add the skate wings and simmer for 15 minutes. Turn off the heat, and leave the wings to cool in the court-bouillon.

≫ Peel the pumpkin and cut into chunks. Wash the apples and cut into chunks. Peel and chop the garlic. Peel and slice the remaining onions.

≫ In a frying pan, sweat the garlic and onions with half of the olive oil for 5 minutes. Add the chopped pumpkin, saffron, and season with salt and pepper. Cook for 10 minutes on medium heat, stirring frequently. Add the chopped apple, honey, and 7 tablespoons of water. Mix well and continue to cook for 6–8 minutes.

≫ Dry-roast the almonds for 3–4 minutes in a non-stick frying pan.

≫ Drain the skate wings, remove the skin, and carefully remove the meat.

≫ Pre-heat the oven to 350 °F (180 °C).

≫ Spread out the skate meat in a large ovenproof dish. Around it, arrange the saffron-flavored pumpkin and its juices along with the almonds. Drizzle all over with the remaining olive oil. Cover the dish with wax paper.

≫ Bake the tagine for 15–20 minutes. Serve piping hot.

ROAST MACKEREL WITH CIDER AND SMOKED SAUSAGE

PREPARATION : 30 minutes
COOKING TIME : 35 minutes

INGREDIENTS

Serves 6

- 6 mackerel, medium size
- 1 bottle cider (750 ml)
- generous 1 lb (500 g) smoked sausage
- 2¼ lb (1 kg) Brussels sprouts
- 1¼ cups (300 ml) heavy cream
- 3½ tbsp (50 g) butter
- salt, ground pepper

》 Pre-heat the oven to 390 °F (200 °C).

》 Cut off the mackerel heads. Gut them, rinse well under cold running water, and pat dry with a clean cloth. Season with salt and pepper and place them in a large ovenproof dish.

》 In a pan, fast-boil the cider with some salt and pepper for 5 minutes. Leave to cool, then pour it over the mackerel.

》 Cover the dish with aluminum foil and bake for 15 minutes.

》 Meanwhile, wash the sprouts. Cook in a pan of boiling, salted water for 12–15 minutes. Drain and rinse under cold water.

》 Take the mackerel out of the oven (but keep it on at 300 °F/ 150 °C). Strain the cooking cider through a sieve and pour it into a pan; reduce by half on medium heat. Add the cream and cook for another 8–10 minutes until the sauce is thick and creamy. Whizz with a hand blender until silky smooth.

》 Remove the sausage skin. Cut the sausage into thick slices, then cut each slice into quarters.

》 Heat the butter in a frying pan and brown the sprouts for 3 minutes on medium heat. Add the sausage, turn up the heat, and brown for 3 minutes on high heat.

》 Put the mackerel back in the oven to heat up for 5 minutes. Serve immediately with the cider sauce, Brussels sprouts, and sausage.

PREPARATION: **45 minutes**
COOKING TIME: **15 minutes**

SQUID WITH CAPERS

INGREDIENTS

Serves 6

- 12 small (or 6 medium) squid
- 2 oz (60 g) capers
- 2 slices sandwich loaf, crusts removed
- scant 1 cup (100 g) Pecorino cheese, grated
- 1¾ oz (50 g) pitted black olives
- 9 tbsp (70 g) pine nuts
- 6 tbsp (50 g) raisins
- 4 shallots
- 2 cloves garlic
- 3 tbsp milk
- 7 tbsp (100 ml) olive oil
- salt, ground pepper

》 Wash the squid. Keep the tubes intact and cut off the tentacles.

》 Soak the bread in the milk.

》 Roughly chop the olives, capers, pine nuts, and raisins. Peel and chop the shallots and garlic.

》 In a frying pan, sweat the shallots and garlic for 3 minutes with half of the olive oil. Add the squid tentacles and brown for 3 minutes. Mix in the chopped capers, olives, pine nuts, and raisins. Continue to cook for 2 minutes, stirring all the time. Transfer the mixture to a bowl and leave it to cool. Add the bread soaked in milk, the Pecorino cheese, salt, and pepper. Mix well.

》 Pre-heat the oven to 390 °F (200 °C).

》 Using a spoon, stuff the squid tubes with the mixture. Close up the ends with a wooden cocktail stick.

》 In a frying pan, sear the stuffed squid for 1 minute on each side in the remaining olive oil; season with salt and pepper. Place them in an ovenproof dish and drizzle with the oil from the frying pan. Bake for 10–15 minutes, depending on the size of the squid, turning them over half way through the cooking time.

》 Remove the squid from the oven and leave them to rest for 5 minutes covered with aluminum foil. Serve with fried rice or buttered linguine.

POLLOCK PIE WITH OLIVES

PREPARATION : 40 minutes
COOKING TIME : 30 minutes

INGREDIENTS
Serves 6

- 2¼ lb (1 kg) pollock fillet
- 2¾ lb (1.2 kg) potatoes
- 1 large onion
- 7 tbsp (100 ml) olive oil
- 1 small sprig rosemary
- salt, ground pepper
- 7 tbsp (100 ml) milk
- 9 tbsp (130 g) butter
- 5½ oz (150 g) small black Niçoise olives
- 3½ oz (100 g) breadcrumbs

≫ Peel and wash the potatoes, then cut them into chunks. Cook for 20 minutes in a pan of boiling, salted water.

≫ Cut the pollock into portions and remove the bones.

≫ Peel and slice the onion. Pick off the rosemary leaves and chop them up.

≫ In a frying pan, sweat the onion for 5 minutes in 2 tablespoons of olive oil. Add the pollock portions, the rosemary, salt, and pepper. Cook for 6–8 minutes on medium heat.

≫ Drain the potatoes and mash them in a bowl until nice and smooth.

≫ In a pan, warm up the milk with the rest of the olive oil and pour the mixture onto the potato mash. Add 7 tablespoons of diced butter and mix well. Fold in the roughly chopped olives.

≫ Pre-heat the oven to 350 °F (180 °C).

≫ Flake the fish and spread it out in a gratin dish along with the onion. Cover with the olive and potato mash. Sprinkle the breadcrumbs on top, and dot with the remaining butter, finely diced.

≫ Bake the gratin in the oven for 25–30 minutes. Serve piping hot.

ROAST TURBOT IN BACON, WITH LETTUCE AND PEAS

PREPARATION: **40 minutes**
COOKING TIME: **20 minutes**

INGREDIENTS
Serves 6

- 6 turbot portions, approx. 8 oz (250 g) each
- 6 little gem lettuce
- salt, ground pepper
- 18 thin slices pork belly (salt pork)
- 6 tbsp (90 g) butter
- 3 tbsp olive oil
- 1 onion
- 1¼ lb (600 g) fresh young peas, shelled
- 1 tbsp caster sugar

≫ Pre-heat the oven to 375 °F (190 °C).

≫ Wash the lettuce and blanch for 2 minutes in a pan of boiling, salted water. Drain and rinse in very cold water; squeeze gently to extract as much water as possible.

≫ Season the fish with salt and pepper. Wrap 3 slices of pork around each portion.

≫ Place the turbot and lettuce in a large ovenproof dish. Season the lettuce with salt and pepper. Dot the fish and lettuce with 4 tablespoons of finely diced butter and drizzle with olive oil. Bake for 15–20 minutes.

≫ Meanwhile, peel and slice the onion. Sweat for 5 minutes in a pan with the remaining butter. Add the peas, sugar, and some salt and pepper. Cover with wax paper and cook for 10–12 minutes on medium heat: the peas should remain crunchy.

≫ Remove the turbot from the oven and serve with the peas.

SEA BREAM IN HERB SALT CRUST

INGREDIENTS

Serves 6

- 2 sea bream, each weighing around
  2 lb (800–900 g)
- 4 sprigs thyme
- 2 sprigs rosemary
- 3 oz (80 g) pink peppercorns
- 4½ lb (2 kg) coarse sea salt
- generous 1 ¹/₃ cups (200 g)
  all-purpose flour
- 12 egg whites

≫ Pre-heat the oven to 350 °F (180 °C). De-scale and gut the sea bream (or ask your fish retailer to do this); rinse well under cold running water, then pat dry with a clean cloth.

≫ Remove the stalks from the thyme and rosemary. Put the leaves in a food grinder with the peppercorns and whizz for 30 seconds.

≫ Put the sea salt and flour in a bowl. Add the herb mixture then fold in the egg whites, making it into a thick paste. Divide the paste into 4.

≫ Line 2 baking sheets with waxed paper and spread 1 portion of paste over each sheet. Place 1 sea bream on each sheet then cover with the remaining salt paste, making sure the fish are completely sealed inside the paste.

≫ Bake the sea bream for 40–45 minutes. Remove from the oven and leave them to rest for 10 minutes.

≫ Carefully break open the salt crust and remove the fillets. Serve immediately with lemon or mint-flavored hollandaise sauce.

Ideally, make the salt paste in a food processor with a dough hook at medium speed. You can flavor the salt with sage, fennel, or cumin seeds, or other herbs and spices.

PREPARATION : 30 minutes
COOKING TIME : 15 minutes

ROAST MONKFISH WITH MUSHROOMS AND HAZELNUTS

INGREDIENTS

Serves 6

- 2¼ lb (1 kg) monkfish fillet
- scant 3 lb (1.2 kg) ceps
- generous ¾ cup (200 ml) meat stock
- 2 large shallots
- 7 tbsp (60 g) whole hazelnuts
- salt, ground pepper
- 3 tbsp hazelnut (or walnut) oil

≫ Pre-heat the oven to 350 °F (180 °C).

≫ Brush the ceps and rinse briefly under cold running water; slice them.

≫ Boil the meat stock in a pan for 5 minutes to reduce it slightly.

≫ Peel and chop the shallots. Roughly crush the hazelnuts.

≫ Heat the nut oil in a frying pan and sweat the shallots for 3 minutes on medium heat. Add the ceps and hazelnuts. Season with salt and pepper, increase the heat, and cook for 6–8 minutes, stirring frequently. Transfer the mixture to an ovenproof dish.

≫ Cut the monkfish fillet into 6 portions and season with salt and pepper. Sear the fish portions in a hot frying pan with some olive oil for 2–3 minutes on each side.

≫ Place the monkfish on the layer of mushrooms, then pour on the meat stock. Bake in the oven for 15 minutes.

≫ Serve the monkfish and mushrooms piping hot, with potato purée made with hazelnut oil.

HAKE PARCELS WITH PANCETTA AND PARMESAN

PREPARATION : 45 minutes
COOKING TIME : 20 minutes

INGREDIENTS
Serves 6

- 6 chunky hake portions, each a generous 6 oz (180 g)
- 5½ oz (150 g) Parmesan
- 6 sage leaves
- 12 slices pancetta
- salt, ground pepper
- $^2/_3$ cup (150 ml) fish stock (see recipe p. 12)
- 7 tbsp (100 ml) white wine
- 3 tbsp olive oil

》 Pre-heat the oven to 390 °F (200 °C).

》 Coarsely grate the Parmesan. Chop the sage.

》 Make a horizontal cut through the middle of the hake portions, creating a pocket. Spread the grated Parmesan and chopped sage on the insides.

》 Place 1 slice of pancetta on the work surface. Put 1 hake portion on top, then cover with another slice of pancetta. Tie the hake up in a parcel with kitchen twine. Season with salt and pepper. Make the other parcels in the same way. Place them in an ovenproof dish.

》 Boil the white wine in a pan for 2 minutes. Add the fish stock and bring back to a boil for 2 minutes. Season with salt and pepper. Pour the mixture into the bottom of the dish and drizzle some olive oil over the fish parcels.

》 Cover the dish with aluminum foil. Bake in the oven for 10–12 minutes.

》 Remove the foil and cook the parcels for another 8–10 minutes. Serve immediately with creamy celeriac mash.

Roast cod with smoked mozzarella and tomato

PREPARATION: **20 minutes**
COOKING TIME: **15 minutes**

INGREDIENTS
Serves 6

- 6 chunky cod fillets, each a
  generous 6 oz (180 g)
- 7 tbsp (100 ml) olive oil
- 6 small vine tomatoes
- generous 1 lb (500 g) smoked
  mozzarella
- salt, ground pepper
- 1 sprig rosemary
- 6 tbsp (90–95 ml) balsamic
  vinegar

》 Pre-heat the oven to to 390 °F (200 °C).

》 In a frying pan, sear the cod fillets in 2 tablespoons of olive oil for 1 minute on each side. Transfer them to an ovenproof dish.

》 Wash the tomatoes, remove the stalks, and cut them into 2-inch- (5-cm-) thick slices.

》 Cut the mozzarella into 3-inch- (7–8-cm-) thick slices.

》 Season the cod fillets with salt and pepper. Place 2 or 3 tomato slices on each fillet, then mozzarella slices, and the rest of the tomatoes. Sprinkle with rosemary leaves and drizzle with olive oil. Bake for 12–15 minutes.

》 Remove the dish from the oven and drizzle 1 tablespoon of balsamic vinegar over each cod fillet. Serve immediately.

Serve this dish with egg-plant and Parmesan gratin.

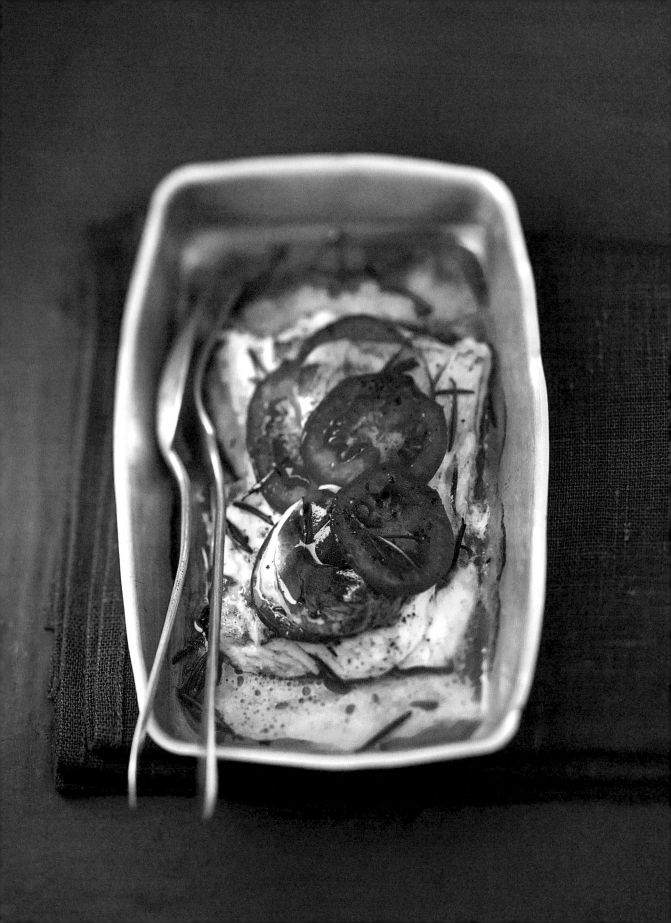

ROAST SEA BASS WITH HERBS AND GARLIC

PREPARATION : 20 minutes
COOKING TIME : 25 minutes

INGREDIENTS

Serves 6

- 3 whole sea bass, each weighing approx. 2 lb (800—900 g)
- 1 whole head of garlic
- 2 large sprigs rosemary
- 1 bunch fresh thyme
- 1 bunch savory
- 6 bay leaves
- 7 tbsp (100 ml) olive oil
- sea salt, ground pepper

≫ Pre-heat the oven to 350 °F (180 °C).

≫ De-scale and gut the sea bass, then rinse thoroughly under cold running water.

≫ Peel and slice the garlic cloves. Blanch them in a pan of boiling, salted water for 20 seconds, then drain.

≫ Rinse all of the herbs. Remove the stalks and chop up the leaves using scissors. Also cut up the bay leaves very finely. Combine them all in a bowl with half of the olive oil.

≫ Season the sea bass cavities with sea salt and pepper. Fill them with half of the chopped herbs. Place the fish in a large ovenproof dish. Spread the rest of the herbs around them, and drizzle with the remaining oil. Season with salt and pepper.

≫ Bake the sea bass in the oven for 10 minutes. Remove the dish from the oven and spread the garlic slices around the fish. Return to the oven for 10—15 minutes. Serve immediately with hollandaise sauce (see recipe p. 10) or beurre blanc (see recipe p. 11).

PREPARATION : 45 minutes
COOKING TIME : 10 minutes

ROASTED SARDINES WITH ONION COMPOTE

INGREDIENTS

Serves 6

- 12 medium size fresh sardines
- 3 red onions
- 2½ tbsp (40 g) butter
- 7 tbsp (100 ml) edible argan (or other nut) oil
- salt, ground pepper
- generous ¾ cup (120 g) whole almonds, shelled
- 2 tbsp crème de cassis or blackcurrant syrup
- 2 tbsp liquid honey
- 3½ oz (100 g) black olives, pitted

≫ Cut the heads off the sardines. Cut open the sardines along the back, butterfly-style: slide a sharp knife along the fillets but do not detach from the tail and then cut out the spine with heavy kitchen scissors. Gut and rinse the sardines well, then pat them dry on paper towels and put them in the refrigerator.

≫ Peel and slice the onions. Sweat them in a large frying pan with the butter and one third of the oil for 20 minutes on low heat. Season with salt and pepper. Add the almonds, crème de cassis, and honey. Mix well and continue to cook for 10 minutes. Combine the roughly chopped olives towards the end of the cooking time.

≫ Pre-heat the oven to 390 °F (200 °C).

≫ Place the sardines, opened out flat, on a baking sheet lined with wax paper. Season with salt and pepper, and drizzle with the rest of the oil. Spread the onion compote on top of the sardines.

≫ Bake the sardines for 8–10 minutes. Serve immediately.

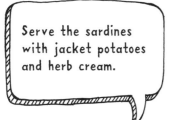

Serve the sardines with jacket potatoes and herb cream.

PREPARATION : 20 minutes
MARINADE : 2 hours
COOKING TIME : 20 minutes

INGREDIENTS
Serves 6

- 2 thick plaice, each approx. 2 lb (800 g–1 kg)
- generous 1 tsp hot curry powder
- generous 1 tbsp cumin seeds
- generous 1 tbsp caraway seeds
- 2 pinches ground cinnamon
- 2 pinches grated nutmeg
- salt, ground pepper
- $^2/_3$ cup (150 ml) olive oil

SPICY ROAST PLAICE

≫ Cut the heads off the fish. Gut them, and rinse well under cold running water. Cut each plaice into 3 thick slices.

≫ In a large bowl, mix together all the spices with salt and pepper. Beat in the olive oil.

≫ Put the plaice slices in the bowl and coat them with the spice mix, turning them carefully with your hands. Cover in plastic wrap and put the bowl in the refrigerator for 2 hours.

≫ Pre-heat the oven to 390 °F (200 °C).

≫ Put the marinated plaice slices in a large ovenproof dish, skin side down, and drizzle with the spicy marinade. Bake in the oven for 15–20 minutes depending on the thickness, drizzling with the spicy oil once or twice during cooking time: the flesh should come away easily from the bone. Serve immediately.

ROAST TROUT WITH ALMONDS AND SORREL EMULSION

PREPARATION : 30 minutes
COOKING TIME : 15 minutes

INGREDIENTS
Serves 6

- 6 medium size trout
- 2 bunches sorrel
- 7 tbsp (100 g) butter
- juice of 1 lemon
- 1 tsp caster sugar
- 7 tbsp (100 ml) fish stock
  (see recipe p. 12)
- 1 ²/₃ cups (400 ml) heavy cream
- salt, ground pepper
- ²/₃ cup (150 ml) white wine
- 1 ¹/₃ cups (200 g) whole almonds,
  shelled
- 4 shallots

> Remove the sorrel stalks and wash the leaves. Sweat the leaves in a pan with 1½ tablespoons of butter on medium heat. Add the lemon juice and sugar. Cook for 2 minutes. Pour in the fish stock and cream, and season with salt and pepper. Bring to a boil and cook for 10 minutes on medium heat until the sauce thickens slightly.

> Pre-heat the oven to 375 °F (190 °C).

> Gut the trout and rinse well under cold running water, then pat dry with a clean cloth. Place them on a baking tray lined with wax paper. Season with salt and pepper.

> Boil the wine in a pan for 5 minutes. Whip in the rest of the butter and season with salt and pepper. Turn off the heat.

> Peel and slice the shallots. Spread the almonds and shallots around the fish. Pour the butter and white wine over the dish, ensuring the trout are well covered. Bake in the oven for 12–15 minutes.

> Using a hand blender, whizz the sorrel sauce until smooth and creamy. Check the seasoning.

> Place 1 trout on each plate with some almonds and shallots. Carefully pull off the skin from the top of the fish and serve immediately with the sorrel sauce.

As an accompaniment, serve with creamy celeriac purée or creamed spinach.

Oysters gratin with mushroom and Parmesan cream

PREPARATION : **40 minutes**
COOKING TIME : **5 minutes**

INGREDIENTS

Serves 6

- 36 oysters (approx. 2–2½ oz/ 60–70 g each)
- 14 oz (400 g) cep mushrooms
- 1 large shallot
- 1½ tbsp (20 g) butter
- salt, ground pepper
- generous ¾ cup (90 g) freshly grated Parmesan
- 1 cup (250 ml) heavy cream

》 Carefully prise open the oysters over a pan. Separate the flesh from the shells and put in the pan. Heat steadily until they just begin to simmer. Drain the oysters in a fine sieve. Strain the juice. Scrub the oyster shells.

》 Brush the mushrooms and rinse them briefly under cold running water. Dice them finely.

》 Peel and chop the shallot. Sweat for 3 minutes in a pan with the butter. Add the mushrooms and season with some salt and pepper. Cook for 5 minutes on medium heat.

》 Scoop half of the mushrooms out of the pan and put them to one side.

》 Pour 3½ tablespoons (50 ml) of the oyster cooking juices into a pan along with the cream. Cook for 8–10 minutes.

》 Whizz the sauce with a hand blender until the mushroom cream is siky smooth. Remove from the heat, stir in the grated Parmesan, and leave it to cool.

》 Pre-heat the oven broiler.

》 Divide the diced mushrooms you left to one side between the empty shells. Place 1 oyster in each shell and cover with the mushroom cream. Brown the oysters for 5 minutes in the broiler. Serve immediately.

MEAT-STUFFED MUSSELS

PREPARATION: **40 minutes**
COOKING TIME: **40 minutes**

INGREDIENTS
Serves 6

- 24 large fresh mussels in shells
- 2 medium onions
- 2 cloves garlic
- 7 tbsp (100 ml) olive oil
- 1 small bunch flat-leaf parsley
- 1¼ lb (600 g) sausage meat
- salt, ground pepper
- 1 quart (1 liter) passata

» Wash the mussels in several changes of water, and drain them in a sieve.

» Peel and chop 1 onion and the garlic cloves. Sweat for 8–10 minutes in a frying pan with half of the olive oil.

» Wash and chop the parsley.

» In a bowl, mix the sausage meat with the softened onion, garlic, and parsley. Season with salt and pepper.

» Carefully open the mussels without separating the two shells. Put a large knob of stuffing in each one, then gently press them closed and tie with kitchen twine.

» Pre-heat the oven to 350 °F (180 °C).

» Peel and chop the second onion. Sweat for 5 minutes in the remaining oil in a dish suitable for both oven and stovetop. Pour on the passata, add a small glass of water, and season with salt and pepper. Bring to a boil and cook for 5 minutes.

» Place the stuffed mussels in the dish with the sauce. Bake in the oven for 35–40 minutes, turning the mussels half way through the cooking time. Serve immediately with rice pilaf.

SHELLFISH GRATIN WITH PARMESAN LEEKS

PREPARATION: 1 hour
COOKING TIME: 10 minutes

INGREDIENTS

Serves 6

- 3¼ lb (1½ kg) mussels
- 3¼ lb (1½ kg) cockles
- 12 scallops, with coral
- 4 large leeks, white parts only
- 1 celery stick
- 1 onion
- 6 tbsp (90 g) butter
- ²/₃ cup (150 ml) white wine
- salt, ground pepper
- 2 tbsp (20 g) cornstarch
- 7 tbsp (100 ml) heavy cream
- scant 1¼ cups (130 g) freshly grated Parmesan
- 2 tbsp olive oil

≫ Wash the mussels and cockles thoroughly.

≫ Peel and chop the onion. Wash and slice the white parts of the leek. Trim and dice the celery finely.

≫ In a large casserole pan, sweat the onion and celery in 1½ tablespoons (20 g) of butter for 2 minutes. Add the shellfish, white wine, and pepper. Cover the pan and cook for 8–10 minutes on high heat, stirring half way through the cooking time. Leave to cool before removing the meat from the shells.

≫ Strain 1¼ cups (300 ml) of the cooking juices and leave to cool.

≫ In a pan, stew the leeks in 3½ tablespoons (50 g) of butter for 15 minutes on medium heat. Season with salt and pepper.

≫ Meanwhile, melt the rest of the butter gently in a small pan. Add the cornstarch and cook for 3 minutes, stirring well to make a roux. Pour in the cooking juices and the cream. Bring to a boil and cook for 3 minutes on medium heat, stirring continuously. Add salt if required, and a little pepper. Remove the pan from the heat and mix in half of the Parmesan. Leave the béchamel sauce to cool.

≫ In a frying pan, sear the scallops in the olive oil for 30 seconds on each side. Season with salt and pepper.

≫ Pre-heat the oven broiler. Spread the soft leeks in the bottom of 6 individual ovenproof dishes. Place 2 whole scallops and some shellfish on top. Coat in the béchamel sauce and smooth over the surface. Sprinkle with grated Parmesan.

≫ Brown the dishes for 10 minutes in the broiler. Serve immediately.

PREPARATION: **45 minutes**
RESTING TIME: **1 hour**
COOKING TIME: **10 minutes**

GINGER CLAMS GRATIN

INGREDIENTS

Serves 6

- 36 large clams
- 1¾ oz (50 g) ginger
- 3 large shallots
- 1 tsp coriander seeds
- 14 tbsp (200 g) butter, room temperature
- 3 tbsp sweet soy sauce
- salt, ground pepper
- 3½ oz (100 g) breadcrumbs
- coarse sea salt

≫ Wash the clams in a basin of cold water, changing it several times, and then drain them in a sieve. Open them carefully so that the flesh remains intact in each shell.

≫ Peel and finely grate the ginger. Peel and chop the shallots. Crush the coriander seeds.

≫ In a large bowl, mix the softened butter with the ginger, shallots, coriander, soy sauce, salt, and pepper.

≫ Drain off the excess juice from the clam shells, and dot with 1 teaspoon of ginger butter. Sprinkle the top with breadcrumbs.

≫ Put the stuffed clams on a baking tray lined with a bed of coarse sea salt to keep them flat. Chill in the refrigerator for at least 1 hour.

≫ Pre-heat the oven broiler and brown the clams for 10 minutes. Serve immediately.

OYSTER GRATIN WITH HORSERADISH

PREPARATION : 40 minutes
COOKING TIME : 5 minutes

INGREDIENTS
Serves 6

- 36 oysters (approx. 2–2½ oz/ 60–70 g each)
- 2 medium size carrots
- 2 celery sticks
- 10 egg yolks
- generous 1 tbsp grated horseradish (jar)
- 3 tbsp white wine
- 2 tbsp (30 g) butter
- salt, ground pepper

≫ Carefully open the oysters over a pan. Separate the flesh from the shells and put in the pan. Heat steadily until the oysters just start to simmer. Drain in a fine sieve.

≫ Peel the carrots and trim the celery; dice them all finely. Put them in a pan, season with salt and pepper, and cook for 10–15 minutes in the butter. They should still be slightly crunchy.

≫ Divide the cooked, diced vegetables between 6 individual heatproof dishes. Put 6 poached oysters in each dish.

≫ Pre-heat the oven broiler.

≫ In a pan, combine the egg yolks with the white wine, and season with salt and pepper. Cook on VERY low heat, beating continuously for about 10 minutes until you have a creamy, light frothy sauce. It is important that the temperature is not too high.

≫ Remove the pan from the heat, and keep beating for 5 minutes to stop the cooking process. Now fold in the horseradish.

≫ Pour the sauce evenly over the poached oysters. Brown them for 4–5 minutes in the broiler. Serve immediately.

LANGOUSTINES WITH ANGEL HAIR PASTA AND VANILLA

PREPARATION: **30 minutes**
COOKING TIME: **5 minutes**

INGREDIENTS

Serves 6

- 18 large langoustines
- 2/3 cup (150 ml) medium sweet white wine
- 3 tbsp white wine vinegar
- 1½ tbsp (20 g) caster sugar
- 1 vanilla pod
- 7 tbsp (100 ml) sunflower oil
- salt, ground pepper
- 5½ oz (150 g) angel hair pasta (from Asian or Middle Eastern grocers)

》 Pre-heat the oven to 390 °F (200 °C).

》 Pour the wine and vinegar into a pan. Add the sugar. Split the vanilla pod lengthways and scrape out the seeds with the tip of a knife. Put them in the pan with the pod. Boil for 5 minutes on medium heat. Leave to cool.

》 Remove the vanilla pod and pour the sunflower oil into the pan. Whizz for 20 seconds with a hand blender until the sauce is smooth and then put the pod back in the pan.

》 Carefully remove the langoustine shells, leaving the tail on. Cut open the backs and remove the black veins.

》 Season the langoustines with salt and pepper and then wrap them carefully in the angel hair pasta. Place them on a baking tray lined with wax paper. Drizzle with olive oil.

》 Bake the langoustines in the oven for 4–5 minutes. Serve immediately with the vanilla sauce and a lamb's lettuce salad.

You can also serve the langoustines with a salad of baby leaves and grated raw beetroot.

CRAB CAKES WITH POTATO, GOAT'S CHEESE, AND BACON

PREPARATION: **45 minutes**
COOKING TIME: **45 minutes**

INGREDIENTS

Serves 6

- 9 oz (250 g) crab meat
- generous 1 lb (500 g) potatoes
- 3 tbsp olive oil + a small amount
  for the molds
- salt, ground pepper
- 7 oz (200 g) fresh goat's milk
  cheese
- 1 egg
- 12 slices bacon

≫ Pre-heat the oven to 320 °F (160 °C).

≫ Peel and wash the potatoes, then cut them into thin rounds. Mix them in a bowl with the olive oil and season with salt and pepper.

≫ In another bowl, crumble the goat's cheese with a fork. Add the egg and beat with a whisk. Fold in the crab meat; season with salt and pepper.

≫ Oil 6 tartlet molds with high sides, then line the bottoms with wax paper.

≫ Place 2 slices of bacon criss-crossed on the bottom of each mold, overlapping the top edges. Add a layer of potatoes. Spread on some of the crab mix, and add a layer of potatoes. Keep layering in this way until all the ingredients are used up, finishing with potatoes. Fold the bacon slices over them, and pat it all down gently with your hands.

≫ Bake the crab cakes for 30 minutes.

≫ Remove the cakes from the oven and increase the temperature to 350 °F (180 °C). Carefully transfer the crab cakes from the molds to a baking tray lined with wax paper and put them back in the oven for 15 minutes. Serve immediately with a salad.

You can make this recipe using a large 8-inch- (20-cm-) spring-form pan: spread all the bacon slices across the bottom of the pan, overlapping the top edges.

FISH SOUP

PREPARATION : 45 minutes
COOKING TIME : approx.
1¹/₂ hours

INGREDIENTS
Serves 6–8

- 4½ lb (2 kg) rockfish, red mullet,
  gurnard or scorpion fish
- 6 cloves garlic
- 1 large onion
- 4 tomatoes
- 1¾ lb (800 g) carrots
- 11 oz (300 g) potatoes
- 7 tbsp (100 ml) olive oil
- 2 tbsp tomato purée
- 3 tbsp pastis
- 2 large pinches saffron powder
- 1 level tbsp chili powder
- salt, ground pepper

》 If using small rockfish, simply wash them (do not gut). Gut the other fish and wash well under cold running water; cut them into chunks.

》 Peel and slice the garlic and onion. Wash and quarter the tomatoes. Peel and wash the potatoes and carrots, then cut them into pieces.

》 In a large pot, sweat the onion and garlic in the olive oil for 5 minutes. Add the fish and brown for 5 minutes on high heat. Add the tomatoes, tomato purée, pastis, chili powder, saffron, salt, and pepper. Mix all the ingredients together well and brown for 5 minutes. Finally, add the carrots and potatoes. Cover completely with cold water. Bring to a boil and simmer gently for 1½–1¾ hours, skimming the surface frequently.

》 Whizz the mixture with a hand blender for 5 minutes. Pass the soup through a fine strainer, squeezing as much liquid as possible out of the fish.

》 Pour the fish soup into a pan and bring to a boil, whisking all the time. Check the seasoning. Serve immediately with garlic croutons, some rouille (see recipe p. 10) and grated Gruyère cheese.

CONVERSIONS

LIQUIDS

Metric	American measure	Imperial
5 ml	1 tsp	1 tsp
15 ml	1 tbsp	1 tbsp
35 ml	2½ tbsp	2½ tbsp
65 ml	¼ cup	2 fl oz
125 ml	½ cup	4½ fl oz
250 ml	1 cup	9 fl oz
500 ml	2 cups	17 fl oz
1 liter	4 cups	1 quart

SOLIDS

Metric	American measure	Imperial
30 g	1 oz	1 oz
55 g	2 oz	2 oz
115 g	4 oz	4 oz
170 g	6 oz	6 oz
225 g	8 oz	8 oz
454 g	1 lb	1 lb

OVEN TEMPERATURES

Temperature	° Celsius	° Fahrenheit	Gas mark
Very cool	140 °C	275 °F	1
Cool	150 °C	300 °F	2
Warm	160 °C	325 °F	3
Moderate	180 °C	350 °F	4
Fairly hot	190–200 °C	375–400 °F	5–6
Hot	220 °C	425 °F	7
Very hot	230–240 °C	450–475 °F	8–9

ACKNOWLEDGEMENTS

A big thank you to Aurélie, Adèle, Mathilde, and Laurent at Mango
for this great new title in the series.
To Pierre-Louis, for always giving us beautiful photos...
To Mauviel for the kitchen utensils.
And to VERYCOOK for lending us their wonderful planchas!

It is advisable not to serve dishes that contain raw eggs to very young
children, pregnant women, elderly people, or to anyone weakened by
serious illness. If in any doubt, consult your doctor. Be sure that all the
eggs you use are as fresh as possible.

© Mango, Paris — 2014
Original Title: *Fish & Co! À la Plancha et au Four*
ISBN 978-23-17007-42-2

Editor: Aurélie Cazenave and Mathilde Croizeau
Graphic Design: Laurent Quellet and Julie Mathieu
Photoengraving: Almalthéa
Production: Thierry Dubus and Marie Guibert

© for this English edition: h.f.ullmann publishing GmbH

Translation from French: Ann Drummond in association with
First Edition Translations Ltd, Cambridge, UK

Project management for h.f.ullmann publishing: Isabel Weiler,
Katharina Pferdmenges

Overall responsibility for production: h.f.ullmann publishing GmbH,
Potsdam, Germany

Printed in Slovenia, 2015

ISBN 978-3-8480-0798-1

10 9 8 7 6 5 4 3 2
X IX VIII VII VI V IV III II I

www.ullmann-publishing.com
newsletter@ullmann-publishing.com
facebook.com/ullmann.social